Mug shots are produced at the very outset of the legal process, after an arrest has been made, but before guilt or innocence has been established. It is a fundamental tenet of our criminal justice system that those accused are presumed innocent until proven guilty beyond a reasonable doubt. Over and above this legal presumption stands the reality that people are at times arrested or accused in error and without basis of fact. That a person has been arrested, or even formally charged, is no proof that he or she committed the alleged crime or offense. The purpose of this book is neither to judge the guilt or innocence of those portrayed, nor to criticize them as artists or human beings.

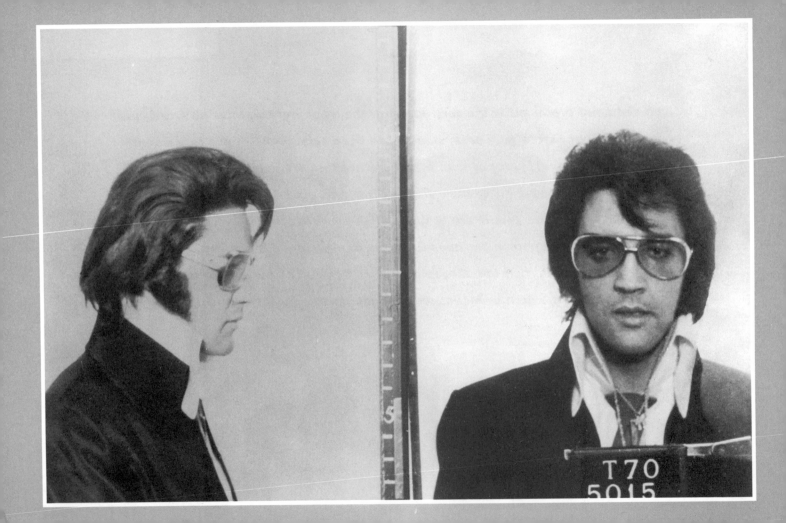

MUG SHOTS

CELEBRITIES UNDER ARREST

Compiled by George Seminara

St. Martin's Griffin New York

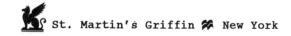

Acknowledgments

I would like to thank the following, without whose help this book would not have been possible: the New York Public Library, the National Archives, the Federal Bureau of Investigation, the Freedom of Information Act, the U.S. Constitution, the hundreds of police agencies across the country that assisted me, Laurie Seminara, Matthew Seminara, Jacob Solotaroff, Ron Wohl, Chris Bongirne, Annabelle Winters, Roger Cooper, Thom Fennessy, my parents and all my in-laws.

It took two years to compile this book, and I would like to thank my friends who helped support me throughout this time: Michele Amatrula, Joey Ramone, John Rae, Cathal Coughlan, Mark Newgarden, Mick Jones, Vincent Giordano, Phil Shuster, Gary Kurfirst and everyone at Radioactive/Overland, Jeff Hieskell, Jeffrey Arch, The Posterboys, Public Pictures, Rat Productions, and Geoff and James at Medialab, London.

I'd like to extend a very special thanks to my agents, Knox Burger and Kitty Sprague, without whose support this book would have remained but a clever idea.

MUG SHOTS: Celebrities Under Arrest

Design by Gretchen Achilles

Seminara, George.
  Mug shots : celebrities under arrest / by George Seminara.
    p. cm.
  ISBN 0-312-14374-5
  1. Criminals-United States-Miscellanea. 2. Celebrities-United
  States-Miscellanea.   I. Title.
  HV6791.S426   1996
364.1'092'273-dc20

First Edition
10 9 8 7 6 5 4 3 2 1

INTRODUCTION   A BRIEF HISTORY OF THE MUG SHOT

The taking of photographs for use in criminal investigations is almost as old as the art form itself. In the late 1800s, law-enforcement agencies typically hired a local photographer to take a portrait of a lawbreaker. In most cases the hired photographer would bring costumes and dress up the subject. Thus very often in early mug shots and wanted posters, the picture would depict a much more refined person than the one the police actually had in custody.

When photography was in its infancy, portrait photographers tried to create an artistic image, a fantasy, that would make for a memorable artistic image. Today, having one's portrait made in a photo studio in an amusement park is as close as one can get to the feel of these early days of crime photography. A person enters, puts on a costume and has his picture taken. One of the only photographs of Billy the Kid is a picture of this type. The full-length image is that of a young man, his hat at a jaunty angle, leaning on his rifle in a rakish pose. It was obviously arranged by the photographer, who was trying harder to get a good shot than a good likeness.

A notable case from mug-shot lore was Charles Julius Guiteau, the man who killed President James Garfield. He shot the president because he had not received a hoped-for appointment as ambassador to France. Just sixteen years after the assassination of President Abraham Lincoln, Guiteau managed to stalk the president openly for months. At one point he was caught roaming the halls of the White House, where he was ejected by Chester A. Arthur, the vice president. Guiteau finally met up with President Garfield on a train platform and shot him in the back. The president died two months later. The assassin became the talk of the country, a celebrity, if you will, as much for his quirky behavior as for the crime he committed.

The police allowed people to view Guiteau in his cell, where he would strut back and forth like a rooster behind the bars. He quickly turned a very serious charge into a show. During his trial, the press printed many of his statements and had artists depict the goings-on inside and outside of court and in jail. Guiteau had many reproductions made of his own mug shots, which he autographed and sold to raise money for his defense. Guiteau even represented himself at his trial. He claimed God told him to kill the president. He cursed the prosecutor and referred to the jury as "consummate jackasses." He insulted virtually everyone with whom he came in contact on his way to the gallows.

The mug shot changed dramatically with the arrival of Alphonse Bertillion's anthropometry in 1882. Bertillion was head of the Criminal Identification Bureau at the Paris Police Department. He felt that no two people could look exactly alike, and that with careful measurements of various body parts—diameter of head, length of right ear, distance of arms outstretched, pinkie size, as well as standing and sitting height—a flawless identification could be made. In 1882. the Bertillion method successfully identified almost fifty criminals who had given false names. Over the next twenty years the Bertillion identification method grew in popularity and success.

During this time, police departments started taking pictures of both the front and profile of their subjects. This was to further aid in identifying the offender and to provide a reference for the Bertillion measurements. On the back of each mug shot was a chart where the arresting officer could fill in these measurements. The Bertillion method wavered when, in the United States, two convicted felons shared identical Bertillion charts. They were later differentiated by a new style of criminal identification: fingerprinting. Because of its greater accuracy, this technique rapidly became the basic means of identifying felons.

The concept of fingerprinting dates back to twelfth-century China. It entered the modern era when Sir Francis Galton's fingerprint classification techniques were adopted, in 1894, by Scotland Yard. Fingerprinting was officially adopted in New York in 1903, and spread across the nation like wildfire, supplanting the Bertillion method by the mid-1920s. Though it is not impossible that two individuals can have the same fingerprint patterns, fingerprint experts rate the possibility to be one in 64 billion.

Another change in police procedure occurred when police departments began to hire their own photographers. These people took photographs of suspects as well as crime scenes. Their intention was to record the subject realistically without any of their predecessors' art direction. These photographs were cold and hard. The modern police photographer takes a basic "Just the facts, ma'am" approach to the subjects. Today, police officers are trained to be photographers, studying lensing and composition. One purpose of the training is to allow the police photographers to create the most calculatedly perfect record of reality. These photographs capture attention by their sheer bluntness. It is the work of these nameless police officers that has created such an emotional impact in high-profile cases like the O. J. Simpson trial.

Today, the tools of recording images by police departments are changing. While some departments rely on the standard film camera with ID board and height chart, many police agencies have switched over to computer-imaging systems. These systems are considered more accurate and therefore no longer require the profile shot. The computer system makes it easier to maintain records by saving everything in computer files, reducing storage space. It also eliminates the need for a darkroom. Finally, it saves money by making photographic copies easier using low-priced computer printers.

Two fine books that explore police photographs are Luc Sante's, <u>Evidence</u> and Inspector Thomas Byrne's <u>Professional</u> <u>Criminals</u> <u>of</u> <u>North</u> <u>America</u>. <u>Evidence</u> is a collection of crime-scene photographs from the early part of this century. All the photos are from the New York Police Department, taken with large-format cameras on glass negatives. It features morbidly beautiful prints and insightful commentary by its author. The second book, <u>Professional</u> <u>Criminals</u> <u>of</u> <u>North</u> <u>America</u>, is much harder to find and is more than one hundred years old. Inspector Thomas Byrnes, who was the chief inspector of detectives for the City of New York, collected, in a single leather-bound edition, countless mug shots and explanations of criminal types and schemes. In 1886, it was the definitive text on the subject.

Many of the famous faces included in this book are among the most pampered by the photographer's art. We have seen these faces in makeup, placed artfully under lights, posed and photographed with every attention to beauty and style. On television, in the cinema, and on magazine covers, these stars have been glamorized. They have been turned into cultural icons, gods and goddesses of our modern mythology. What follows is a gallery of these same artists, shorn of styling and technique, presented, perhaps for the first time, simply as people.

The crimes charged range from drunk driving to murder. Some of the people presented may have thought themselves above or beyond the law, some were merely in the wrong place at the wrong time. <u>Mug</u> <u>Shots</u> is a commentary not on the price of celebrity, but on the price of life in the twentieth century.

INCIDENT REPORT

NAME Tim Allen

ARREST October 2, 1978

LOCATION Kalamazoo, Michigan

CHARGE Delivery of a controlled substance; conspiracy

INCIDENT

Two men drove a year-old, silver Chevy Nova, into the parking lot of the Kalamazoo airport one evening. They were delivering a substantial amount of cocaine to a third man. During the meeting, the three men were surprised to discover that they had fallen into a trap set by Michigan State Police. One of them, Timothy Alan Dick, was taken to the Kalamazoo City Jail. He was interrogated for close to six hours and booked on drug charges. ¶Tim Dick was then placed in a holding cell where he sat for two weeks. On October 17, 1978, he was released on a $100,000 bond. On November 26, 1979, he pleaded no contest to the charges. Judge Patrick H. McCauly, of the Kalamazoo County Circuit Court, sentenced Mr. Dick, to not more than seven, and no less than three years in prison. The judge instructed the twenty-five-year-old prisoner that he should use this time to get his proverbial act together. Mr. Dick was credited forty-four days for his time in the city jail and was led away by officers of the Michigan Department of Corrections. ¶While in prison, Mr. Dick learned to use his natural comedic abilities, to protect himself. He has been quoted as saying, "Humor was the best defense I had." A rare rehabilitation success, Mr. Dick used his prison time to read voraciously and take a public-speaking course. That work helped lay the groundwork for his success as a comedian a few years after his release. ¶Timothy Alan Dick changed his name to Tim Allen and became a headliner on the stand-up comedy circuit. In the 1990s he became the star of his own television series, "Home Improvement." Tim Allen has been one of the only performers in history to have a number-one film, a number-one TV series, and a number-one best-selling book at the same time. "In a hideous way," Mr. Allen has stated, "getting caught probably saved my life."

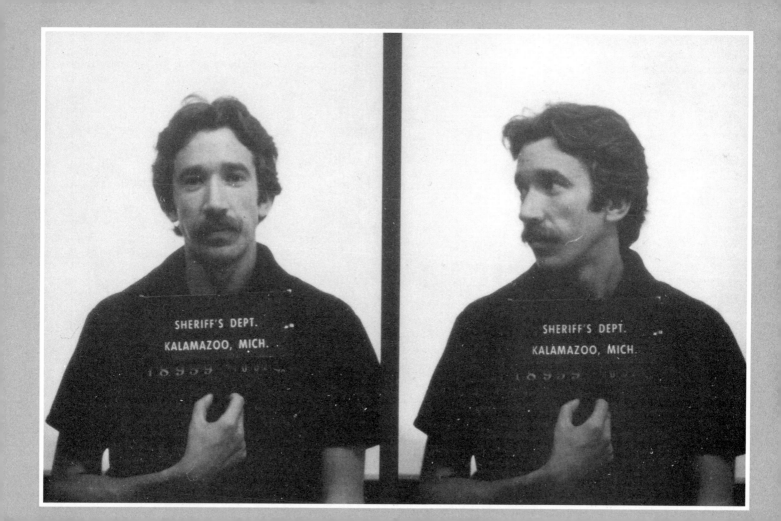

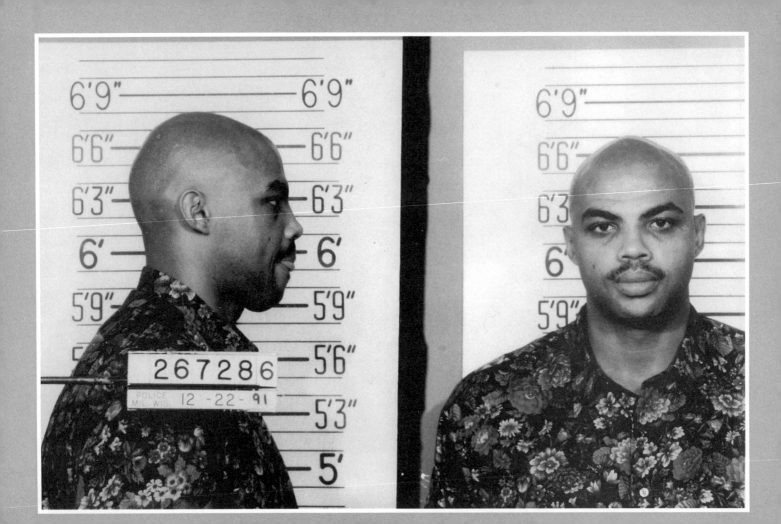

INCIDENT REPORT

NAME Charles Barkley

LOCATION Milwaukee, Wisconsin

ARREST December 21, 1991

CHARGE Battery; disorderly conduct

INCIDENT

Charles Barkley was a player for the Philadelphia 76ers at the time of his arrest. He was apprehended for breaking the nose of a Wisconsin man, Joseph McCarthy. The incident took place early in the morning outside a Milwaukee bar. Barkley maintained that McCarthy had taunted him, yelling "Hey Barkley, show me how tough you are!" as he and a friend left the bar. McCarthy and a group of his friends followed Barkley, allegedly hurling insults at him as they walked. According to the Milwaukee police, McCarthy then raised his fist and challenged him: "Hey, Charles, I hear you're the baddest dude in the NBA." Mr. Barkley terminated the altercation with one perfect punch, flattening his heckler's nose. Charles Barkley was taken into custody at about 7:00 A.M. and charged with battery. He was released on a $500 bond. ¶Barkley was acquitted of all charges after a three-day trial in Milwaukee on June 17, 1992. The jury, which consisted of nine women and three men, were reported to have accepted Barkley's argument that he acted in self-defense when he broke McCarthy's nose. After the verdict was handed down the Philadelphia 76ers announced the trade of Barkley to the Phoenix Suns.

INCIDENT REPORT

NAME Danny Bonaduce

LOCATION Phoenix, Arizona

ARREST March 31, 1991

CHARGE Assault

INCIDENT

The disc jockey and former "Partridge Family" star was arrested after an altercation with a prostitute in the early hours of the morning. Police officers arrived at the scene to find the complainant, someone who appeared to be a woman dressed in a tattered blouse and red miniskirt. The woman was distraught and claimed to have been attacked by Danny "Partridge." Police reports speculated that Mr. Bonaduce pulled over to the curb and invited the prostitute into his car. After allegedly paying the woman for her services (whether said services were provided was not disclosed), Mr. Bonaduce reached under her dress to make a curious discovery: a penis. ¶Police believed that Mr. Bonaduce then grabbed the money out of his/her hand and a struggle ensued. He eventually forced him/her out of his vehicle and made his escape. Mr. Bonaduce's blue Camaro was spotted by a police sergeant who gave chase. Police finally arrested him at his apartment in the St. Croix Villas, on East Fillmore Street. Taken to Memorial Hospital for treatment to his eye, which had been injured during the struggle, Mr. Bonaduce was then booked on assault charges. The victim turned out to be one Darius Lee Barney. ¶The trial became a cause célèbre in Phoenix, where it received front-page coverage in the newspapers. In his testimony Mr. Bonaduce claimed he was just inquiring about the poor soul's condition when the hooker took an unprovoked swing at him. He pleaded no contest and was sentenced to 750 hours of community service. In addition, Mr. Bonaduce paid for plastic surgery to repair Mr. Barney's broken nose.

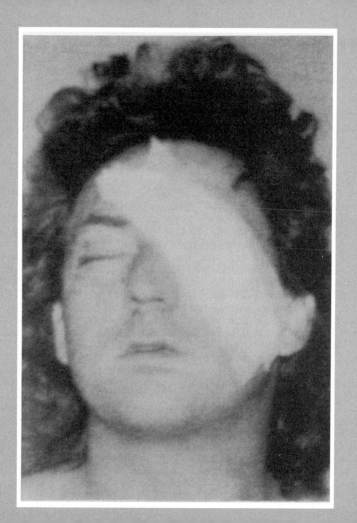

INCIDENT REPORT

NAME Calvin Broadus (Snoop Doggy Dogg)

LOCATION Los Angeles, California

ARREST August 25, 1993

CHARGE Accomplice to murder; manslaughter

INCIDENT

In the early evening, near the corner of Palms Boulevard and Motor Avenue in Los Angeles, three young men in a Jeep got into a heated argument with another man standing on the sidewalk. After some coarse language and a display of gang hand signals, the Jeep sped off. Philip Woldemariam watched the jeep turn the corner. He had recently been released from prison after serving a one year sentence. One of the conditions for his parole was that he stay away from gang members. The Jeep returned and, after another verbal exchange, gun shots were fired. Philip Woldemariam lay dying on the sidewalk. ¶Eyewitnesses identified the driver of the car as Calvin Broadus, better known as Snoop Doggy Dogg. Leery of the LAPD, Snoop had an attorney arrange for him and the two other suspects to surrender to the police on the same night Snoop was set to perform at the MTV Music Video Awards. McKinley Lee, the suspected shooter, and the third suspect arrived at the police station on time. When Snoop failed to show, the department sent officers to the Universal Amphitheater hoping to arrest Mr. Broadus as he left the stage. In the confusion Snoop eluded the police. Escorted by his attorney, David Kenner, Snoop Doggy Dogg entered the police station on his own accord. At his arraignment on Friday, September 3, Snoop faced Judge Lance Ito. During the hearing, police stated that Calvin Broadus, aka Snoop Doggy Dogg, was listed as a member of the L.A. gang called the Crips. In addition, prosecutors charged him for violating laws that prohibit a felon from carrying a firearm. In 1990, Mr. Broadus had been convicted of possessing drugs for sale. ¶Snoop Doggy Dogg pleaded innocent and was released on $1 million bail. At a pretrial hearing, Mr. Kenner, Mr. Broadus's attorney, demanded that all the charges against his client be dropped because police had accidentally destroyed all the physical evidence. Deputy District Attorney Ed Nilson stated that the trial was not based on physical evidence but eyewitness accounts. ¶In February 1996, in yet another high-profile failure for the Los Angeles district attorney's office, a jury found Snoop Doggy Dogg and McKinley Lee not guilty on the charge of murder. The jury deliberated for four days before handing down the verdict on the main count. Two days later, the jury was deadlocked on the lesser count of voluntary manslaughter and a mistrial was declared. The rapper and his bodyguard's bail was reduced from $1 million to $100,000, and they no longer needed to be electronically monitored. The district attorney's office announced that they would soon decide if they would seek a retrial on the manslaughter charge.

INCIDENT REPORT

NAME James Brown

ARREST September 24, 1988

LOCATION Aiken County, South Carolina and Augusta, Georgia

CHARGE Simple assault; carrying a pistol without a license; carrying a deadly weapon at a public gathering; two counts of assault with intent to kill; seven misdemeanor charges

INCIDENT

The people attending an afternoon insurance seminar, were surprised to find James Brown, the "Godfather of Soul," walk in wearing a cowboy hat and brandishing a pistol and a shotgun. "Who used my restroom?" demanded the Hardest-Working Man in Show Business, who kept a business office in the building. Mr. Brown instructed two women to lock the toilet's door and give him the key. He then left the building, got into his late-model red and white pickup truck and sped off. ¶And sped is the right word. Brown was practically flying. The truck was spotted by a Richmond County police officer, who pursued Mr. Brown onto eastbound Interstate 20. As the pickup truck crossed into South Carolina, the chase was picked up by officers from North Augusta, South Carolina. Officers tried to stop Mr. Brown by shooting out the tires of his truck. Even with the vehicle semi-disabled, Mr. Brown drove on the rims through a blockade, turned around, and headed back to Georgia. With several police cars hot on his tail, Mr. Brown drove off the road, where his rims got stuck in the dirt, and he was finally apprehended. The singer was no stranger to the law. Previous charges include possession of the drug PCP, resisting arrest, possession of an unlicensed handgun, and attempted murder (of his wife, Adrienne Brown). Mrs. Brown refused to testify against her husband, and those charges were dropped. ¶At Mr. Brown's trial, Aiken County Judge Hubert E. Long listened to long hours of testimony from friends, family, and fans of James Brown and his music. Court Bailiff George Brown pleaded with the judge, "Give him a chance, Your Honor." The defendant himself told the judge that "James Brown is just a man who wants to do right." Admitting that "the responsibility of passing judgment is not an easy one," Judge Long told the court that he had to consider the community as well as Mr. Brown, then sentenced the singer to six years in the penitentiary, five years of probation with mandatory first-year drug testing, and a $6,000 fine. ¶After two years in prison, James Brown was granted parole by the South Carolina Parole Board.

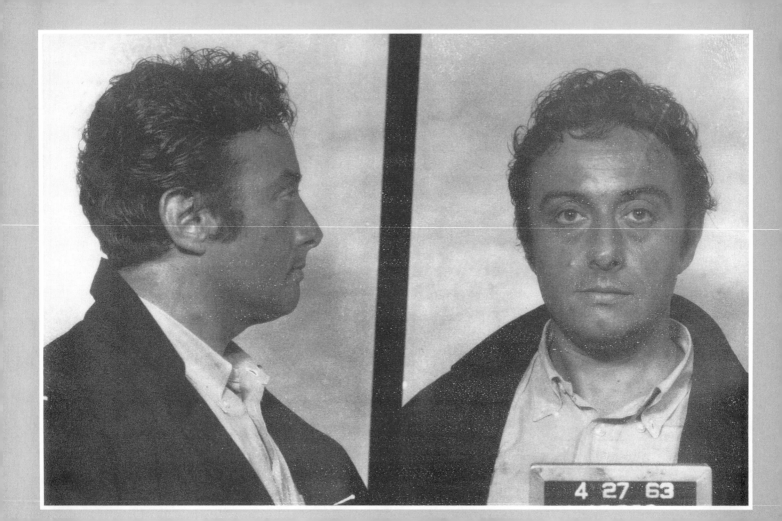

INCIDENT REPORT

NAME Lenny Bruce

ARREST April 27, 1963

LOCATION Miami Beach, Florida

CHARGE Possession of hypodermic needles

INCIDENT

While on routine patrol, Officer J. Booth noted a car with no tail or brake lights. Pursuing the vehicle, which was also speeding, he pulled the late-model Chevrolet to the side of the road near the intersection of Rue Notre Dame and Normandy Drive. The driver stepped out of the automobile and walked over to the patrol car. He handed his driver's license to the officer and went on to tell him the car was rented. Patrolman Booth requested that Mr. Bruce produce the contract for his rental car. While Mr. Bruce rummaged through the auto, Sergeant Griscom and Officer Yawn arrived on the scene. ¶Mr. Bruce informed the officers that he could not find his rental contract. Griscom asked him if he had any more identification or a draft card. Mr. Bruce said that he would have to look in the car for his billfold. While Mr. Bruce was searching through the glove compartment, the officers spotted a sealed hypodermic needle and some vials of an unspecified substance. Mr. Bruce explained to the officers that the vials were not labeled correctly, that the pills contained within were not what the label indicated. He was placed under arrest and a more detailed search of the car revealed two more hypodermic needles. In addition, a wide variety of pills were found in the car on his person. He reportedly had no money with him but was released after posting a $50 bond. ¶Mr. Bruce, a comedian who made stand-up comedy socially relevant, had been arrested once before in Miami Beach in 1951, for panhandling while dressed as a priest. He was arrested several times for obscenity during his nightclub act. On December 21, 1964, he was convicted of obscenity, in Chicago, and sentenced to four months of hard labor. ¶Lenny Bruce died under a cloud of suspicion. On August 3, 1966, his body was found lying in the doorway of a bathroom in his Los Angeles home. Eyewitnesses maintained that police officers moved the body to make it appear that he had died from a drug overdose. The sanctity of the crime scene may have been violated, because police deemed Bruce's death a suicide or death by misadventure. With the absence of evidence to the contrary, journalists were allowed into the house to photograph his corpse.

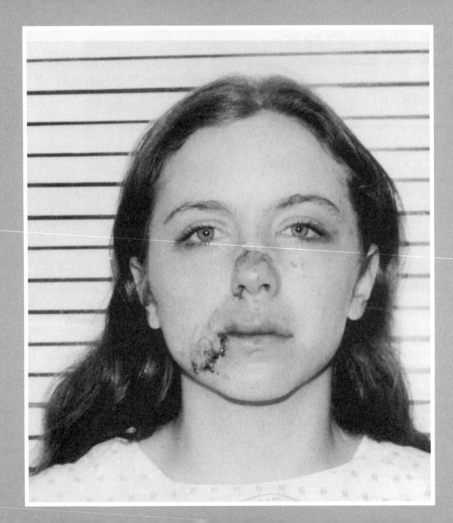

INCIDENT REPORT

NAME Brett Butler

LOCATION Cobb County, Georgia

ARREST May 31, 1981

CHARGE Driving under the influence

INCIDENT

On the evening of May 30, 1981, twenty-three-year-old Brett Butler was returning to her mother's home after attending a concert. She had recently separated from her first husband, Charles Wilson. That night she had been drinking heavily and lost control of her car, smashing into a mailbox and plowing into two trees before coming to a stop. Barely conscious, she was taken by police to Kemmestone Hospital where she was cleaned up and treated for various contusions. From the hospital authorities took her directly to the Cobb County Jail, where she was booked for DUI. Ms. Butler spent the rest of the night in jail. ¶She was released on her own recognizance and ordered to face Cobb County Judge Ray Gary on July 2, 1981. Judge Gary found her guilty of DUI, but sentenced the first-time offender lightly. She was to pay a $250 fine and spend two days in traffic school. Ms. Butler, now the star of the TV show "Grace Under Fire," has spoken of her arrest in many interviews. She has been quoted as affirming, "If talking about it is any help to any other people who drink and drive ... well, good!"

INCIDENT REPORT

NAME Rory Calhoun

ARREST April 23, 1940

LOCATION Salt Lake City, Utah

CHARGE Second-degree burglary; transporting a stolen automobile across state lines

INCIDENT

In the early morning hours, two uniformed officers burst through the front door of a jewelry store and surprised two teenagers who were in the process of robbing it. One of the youths, a seventeen-year-old, yelled, "Run kid, I'll keep them busy!" He engaged both of the officers in a fistfight, allowing the other unidentified youth to escape. Police arrested the remaining youth, who was using the alias "Jack Raine," for second-degree burglary. ¶Salt Lake City police discovered that the prisoner they were holding was wanted by the Los Angeles Police Department on a parole violation stemming from a grand theft auto conviction in 1939. "Jack Raine," who was now known as Francis Macowan, confessed to Salt Lake City police that he was also guilty of violating the Dyer Act, a federal law against transporting a stolen vehicle across state lines. The automobile he had been driving had been stolen in San Francisco a week before his arrest. ¶Francis Macowan was remanded into the custody of the attorney general's office under his real name, Francis Durgin. He was placed into the federal reformatory in El Reno, Oklahoma, under the Juvenile Delinquency Act. While in El Reno, Mr. Durgin was taken under the wing of Father Donald Kanaly. The priest tried to persuade the California authorities to drop the charges against Mr. Durgin, who was facing up to twenty years in San Quentin. California rejected the cleric's pleas and the now twenty-year-old Durgin attempted an escape. Foiled, he was placed in solitary confinement for fourteen days. After his tenure in the "hole," the Federal Prison Board transferred Mr. Durgin to the federal penitentiary in Springfield, Missouri. ¶Father Kanaly never gave up hope on the youth, and eventually persuaded the California authorities to drop charges against him. On his twenty-first birthday, Francis Timothy Durgin walked out of the Springfield Federal Penitentiary a free man. He moved to California and secured work with the Forestry Department. As a park ranger, he became acquainted with Alan Ladd and his wife. The couple were taken by Mr. Durgin's rugged good looks and easygoing manner and decided that he could, with a lot of training, become an actor in Hollywood. The couple fashioned the former convict Francis T. Durgin into the movie star known as Rory Calhoun.

INCIDENT REPORT

NAME Luther Campbell

LOCATION Fort Lauderdale, Florida

ARREST June 10, 1990

CHARGE Obscenity

INCIDENT

Mr. Campbell, the owner of Luke Records, is an extremely successful producer of rap music and the creator of the "Miami Sound." He is also the lead singer of the rap group 2 Live Crew. Mr. Campbell started his recording career by selling a self-produced record, Throw the D, from the trunk of his car. The record sold more than 200,000 copies and earned him enough money to start Skywalker Records and the band 2 Live Crew. The group specializes in raunchy party music, like their anthem "Me So Horny." Mr. Campbell was arrested, along with his 2 Live Crew cohorts, Mark Ross and Chris Wong Won, for performing songs from their album As Nasty as They Wanna Be at an adults-only show at the Futura Night Club in Hollywood, Florida. The album had been ruled obscene two days earlier by Federal District Judge Jose Gonzalez. ¶At the opening of Mr. Campbell's trial, Broward County Sheriff Nick Navarro stated that he hoped the trial would determine if the recording was "protected under the First Amendment or disposable, unprotected smut." ¶During the two-week trial, jurors were played an almost unintelligible recording from the show in question, in which the band performed selections from the album. The lyrics were translated by an officer from the sheriff's department. After close to three hours of testimony, the jurors passed Judge June L. Johnson a note. The note asked if "they, the jury, were allowed to laugh." Judge Johnson said they were and the jury began to laugh through the remainder of the translation. The jurors also listened to expert testimony from John Eland, a music critic from New York, and Duke University Professor Henry Louis Gates, Jr., who called the music in question the work of "literary geniuses." Mr. Campbell and his 2 Live Crew were found not guilty of violating obscenity laws. The jury foreman told the press, "It was just not obscene. People in everyday society use those words." Bruce Rogow, Mr. Campbell's attorney, did not view this case as ground-breaking. "Tomorrow someone can say those same words and still get arrested."

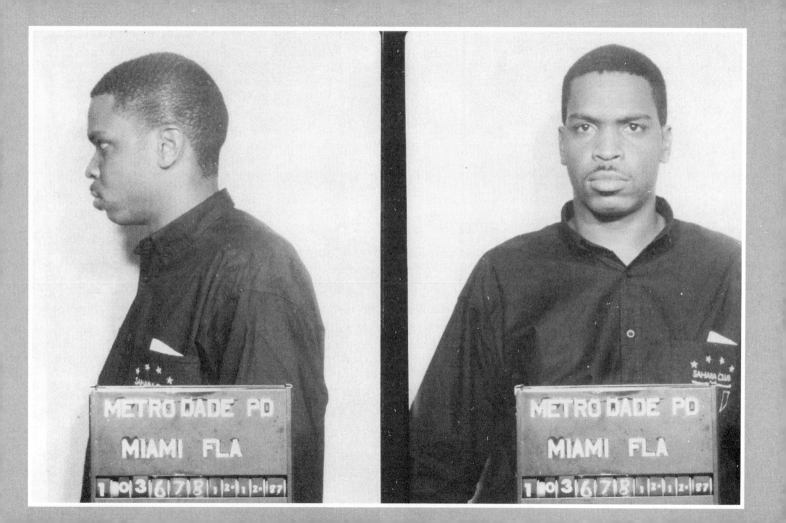

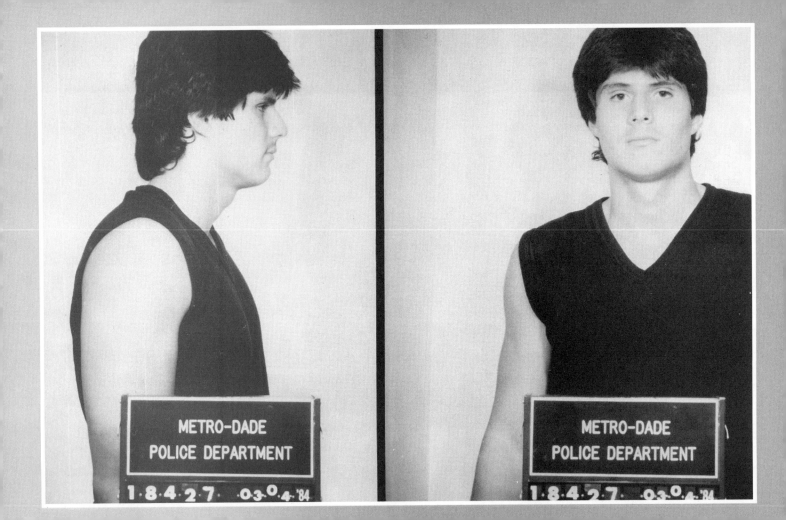

INCIDENT REPORT

NAME Jose Canseco

ARREST March 4, 1984

LOCATION Dade County, Florida

CHARGE Speeding

INCIDENT

Canseco, the 1988 American League MVP, has been arrested for a series of auto-related crimes. In his candy-apple-red Jaguar XJS, he was arrested in Florida several times for speeding; while he was having an MRI performed on his arm at the University of California at San Francisco Medical Center, an unidentified passerby noticed a .9mm handgun on the floor of Canseco's car. As Canseco and his wife were preparing to pull out of the hospital's parking spot, police stopped them. The Cansecos were asked to step away from the vehicle and the loaded gun was taken into police possession. Canseco was arrested for illegal possession of a handgun and released on $2,500 bail. He ultimately pleaded no contest to a misdemeanor of possessing a weapon in an automobile and received a sentence of three years' unsupervised probation. ¶In another incident, Canseco was arrested in his white Porsche for speeding and driving without a license. "I got pulled over for driving thirteen miles over the speed limit," stated the slugger. "Can you believe that?"

INCIDENT REPORT

NAME Jennifer Capriati

ARREST May 16, 1994

LOCATION Coral Gables, Florida

CHARGE Misdemeanor possession of cannabis

INCIDENT

A tip about a runaway seventeen-year-old girl brought the police on a rainy Monday evening in May to an inexpensive motel situated across the street from the University of Miami. Knocking on the door of room 208 of the Gables Inn, police asked its occupant if they could enter. The room's tenant was eighteen-year-old Jennifer Capriati, the tennis phenomenon who had left professional tennis several months earlier to continue high school. A search of the room by the police turned up a small bag of marijuana. Ms. Capriati had rented the room with her credit card, but was not its sole occupant. Within moments after the police arrived, the runaway girl and twenty-year-old Tom Wineland returned to the motel. Mr. Wineland was smoking a crack pipe as he pulled up in Ms. Capriati's car. When Mr. Wineland saw the police, he allegedly shoved the pipe into his pants pocket. The runaway (whose name was withheld) had two packets of heroin on her person, while Mr. Wineland was found to have vials of crack cocaine and other drug paraphernalia in his possession. ¶Ms. Capriati was booked on possession of less than twenty grams of marijuana, a misdemeanor. She was released to her lawyer, John Ross. If convicted, Ms. Capriati could have spent as much as a year in prison. The runaway was released to her mother, while Tom Wineland was held at the Dade County jail because of an outstanding fugitive warrant from Connecticut. In June 1994, Wineland pleaded no contest to possession of crack cocaine and drug paraphernalia and was sentenced to thirty days plus time served. He was ineligible for release, however, because he was wanted by Connecticut authorities for a parole violation on a past drug conviction. ¶Ms. Capriati's lawyer anticipated the judge's sentence: entry into a drug treatment program. As a result, on Wednesday, May 18, two days after the arrest, Ms. Capriati voluntarily entered such a program. No further chargers were brought and none were pressed. In September 1994, Ms. Capriati returned to professional tennis.

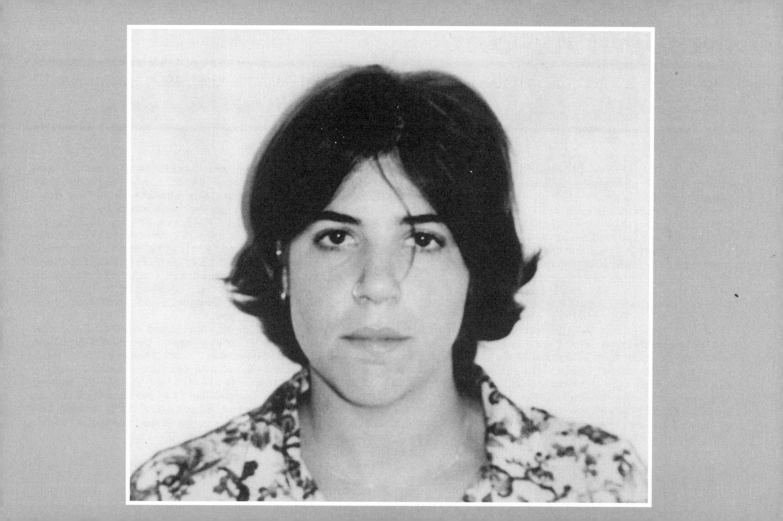

INCIDENT REPORT

NAME George Carlin

ARREST July 21, 1972

LOCATION Milwaukee, Wisconsin

CHARGE Disorderly conduct; obscenity

INCIDENT

At the close of his act at the Summerfest Festival on Lake Michigan, Mr. Carlin was arrested and charged with obscenity and disorderly conduct stemming from the language used in his routine "The Seven Words You Can't Say on TV." Police acted on complaints filed by families who attended the festival, many of whom had small children. The complainants stated that they were shocked by Mr. Carlin's language. He was released on a $150 cash bail. ¶A subsequent radio broadcast of the routine by the Pacifica Foundation in New York City received a civil inquiry by the Federal Communications Commission (FCC). The broadcast was the result of an on-air discussion of society's attitude toward language. Before playing Mr. Carlin's routine, the station warned that the language could offend some listeners. A man who apparently did not hear the warning heard the broadcast while driving with his young son, and complained to the FCC. In response, Pacifica called Mr. Carlin a "significant social satirist" who, "like Twain and Sahl before him, examines the language of ordinary people...." ¶In the criminal case, County Judge Thaddeus Pruss refused the motion to dismiss by Mr. Carlin's attorney, William Coffey. In court, Mr. Coffey declared that Mr. Carlin's use of language was protected under the First Amendment. The judge disagreed, as did the Wisconsin Supreme Court and eventually the U.S. Supreme Court under Chief Justice William Rehnquist, and Justice John Paul Stevens, who ruled in the FCC case that protection could be granted only under provisional guidelines and that the government had the right to regulate broadcasts and performances that were deemed indecent but not obscene. The routine would be limited to and protected by its performance in an adults-only venue. The Carlin-Pacifica First Amendment case is now studied by virtually every law student in America. ¶Twenty-four years later, none of the seven words can be used on television. They are: shit, piss, fuck, cunt, motherfucker, cocksucker, and tits.

132597

INCIDENT REPORT

NAME David Crosby

ARREST April 13, 1982

LOCATION Dallas, Texas

CHARGE Felonious possession of cocaine; illegal possession of a handgun

INCIDENT

After performing in a Dallas night club, David Crosby refused to leave his dressing room. The club's manager was trying to close up, and after numerous attempts to speak with the singer, the manager finally called the police, who arrived to find Mr. Crosby freebasing cocaine while holding a .45-caliber pistol in his lap. He was arrested and was ordered by Dallas Judge Pat MacDowell, under a plea arrangement, to seek rehabilitation. ¶Remanded to the Fair Oaks Hospital Drug Rehabilitation Center in Summit, New Jersey, Mr. Crosby promptly escaped. Arrested the following day in New York City, Mr. Crosby spent the night in New York's Riker's Island Detention Center. At his bail hearing, Mr. Crosby expressed a desire to return to Fair Oaks, and with that proviso, bail was granted. Texas authorities then announced plans to extradite him back to Dallas to serve out his term in prison. Mr. Crosby, to avoid incarceration, disappeared. ¶A national manhunt ensued. Every police agency in the United States received Crosby's description, rap sheet, and the outstanding warrants. Tracked to Miami, Florida, Crosby was arrested several days later in West Palm Beach. Accompanied by an FBI agent, he was extradited to Texas to the Dallas County Jail. Mr. Crosby served eleven months of a five-year sentence there.

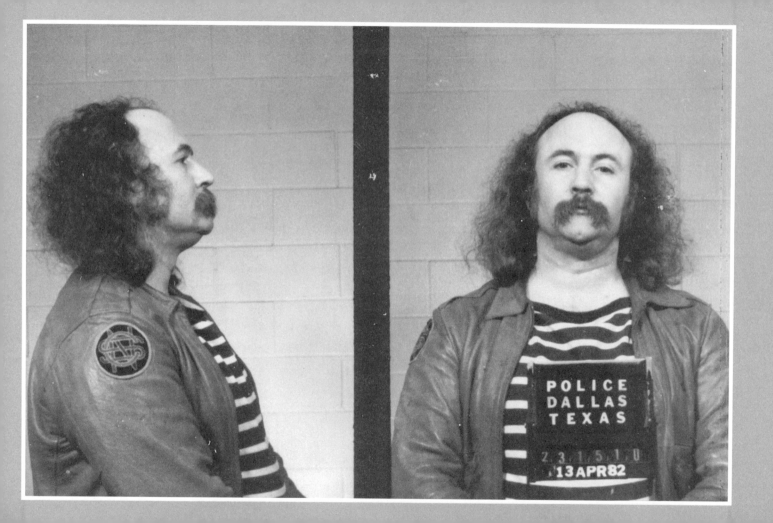

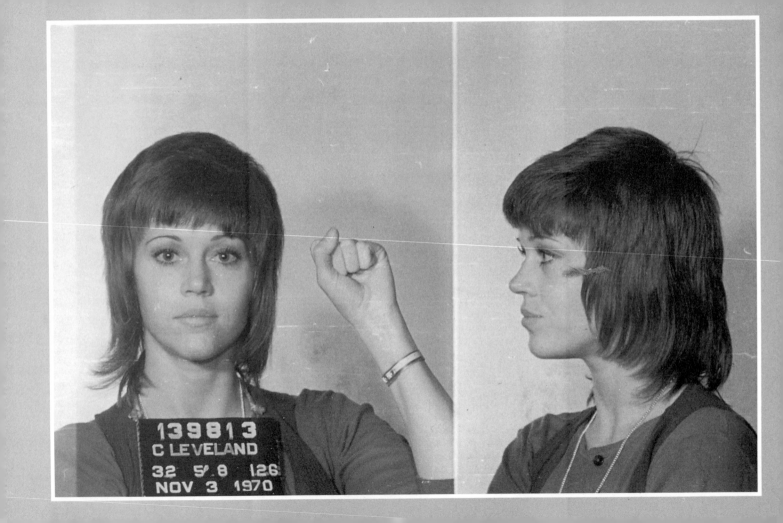

139813
C LEVELAND
32 5 8 126
NOV 3 1970

INCIDENT REPORT

NAME Jane Fonda

ARREST November 3, 1970

LOCATION Cleveland, Ohio

CHARGE Assault and battery

INCIDENT

Ms. Fonda was stopped by U.S. Customs officials at Hopkins International Airport, on her way to a speaking engagement at Bowling Green State College. After a skirmish that involved Ms. Fonda allegedly kicking a policeman and pushing a customs official in an attempt to get to the ladies' room, she was detained. A search of her personal belongings revealed 102 plastic vials. These were filled with health foods and vitamins, as well as one vial each of the prescription drugs Dexedrine, Valium, and Compazine. She was arrested and held at the Cuyahoga County Jail on federal charges of drug smuggling and local charges of assaulting a police officer. Ms. Fonda was arraigned and released on a personal bond of $5,000 and a $500 surety bond. ¶Prior to her release Ms. Fonda was held for three hours in the Cuyahoga jail. While there she met Barbara Kahn, an eighteen-year-old Cleveland girl who had been arrested for disturbing a parade by the United Hard Hats of America. Ms. Kahn told Ms. Fonda of her mistreatment by the Cleveland police. Ms. Fonda felt that Barbara Kahn's treatment was akin to that of a political prisoner. This meeting may have been one of the incidents that encouraged the former Barbarella star to join in the fight for women's rights and become a spokeswoman for feminism worldwide. ¶In the United States of America v. Jane Fonda, Judge Edward F. Fieghan of the Cleveland Municipal Court found in favor of Ms. Fonda, and all charges were dropped when the drugs were identified as legally prescribed pills. Local police asked for a retrial, but this request was dropped after no new evidence could be found. Ms. Fonda in turn dropped her own suit for $100,000 against the Cleveland Police Department for personal injuries.

INCIDENT REPORT

NAME Zsa Zsa Gabor

ARREST June 14, 1989

LOCATION Beverly Hills, California

CHARGE Battery against an officer; disobeying an officer; driving without a registration; driving without a license; driving with an open container of alcohol

INCIDENT

It was a sunny June day as Zsa Zsa Gabor, actress and author of the gold digger's Bible, <u>The Complete Guide to Men</u>, drove her Rolls Royce Corniche through Beverly Hills. A motorcycle police officer, Paul Kramer, appeared alongside the Rolls and directed her to pull over. He then instructed the actress to hand over her license and registration. Ms. Gabor retrieved both items from the glove compartment. Unfortunately, they had both expired. After a ten-minute wait, while Officer Kramer was checking her for priors, Ms. Gabor uttered a few choice words and drove off. Officer Kramer gave chase and pulled Ms. Gabor over again. This time he asked her to step out of the car and she came out swinging, slapping the officer in the face, knocking his regulation sunglasses to the asphalt. ¶Officer Kramer arrested Ms. Gabor and called for back-up to take her to the police station. According to Ms. Gabor's statement, Officer Kramer had handcuffed her so tightly that her wrists were bruised so severely she was unable to attend a charity event that evening. A cursory search of her vehicle turned up a silver flask of bourbon, adding another charge to her arrest. Ms. Gabor was taken to the Beverly Hills police station and booked on five charges. ¶At the station house it was discovered that Ms. Gabor had indeed renewed her registration. However, she had overpaid for it and the ensuing bureaucratic red tape delayed receipt of her new tags. The flask turned out to be the property of Ms. Gabor's eighth husband, Prince Frederick von Anhalt. ¶After leaving the station, Ms. Gabor remarked to assembled reporters that her police experience "was like Nazi Germany." About Officer Kramer, she told <u>People</u> magazine, "You should have seen the hatred in his eyes." As for slapping the officer, she quipped, "I have a Hungarian temper." ¶Later dissatisfied with the trial proceedings in Beverly Hills Municipal Court, which seemed to be heading to a routine sentencing, Ms. Gabor's attorney, Harrison Bull, called six witnesses to support his motion for a new trial. When Judge Charles Rubin denied the motion, Mr. Bull called three witnesses to defend Ms. Gabor's character. Judge Rubin found her guilty of slapping Officer Kramer and of two of the traffic offenses. He then sentenced Ms. Gabor to seventy-two hours in jail, one-hundred-and-twenty hours of community service, and $13,000 in court costs.

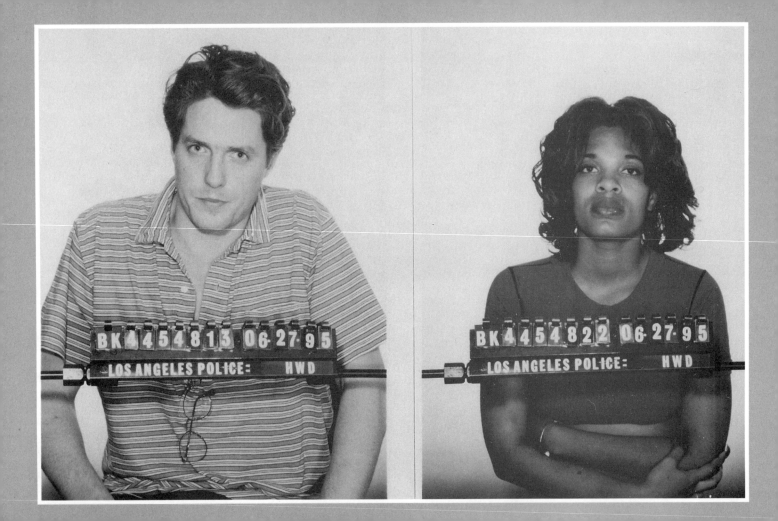

INCIDENT REPORT

NAME Hugh Grant

ARREST June 27, 1995

LOCATION Los Angeles, California

CHARGE Lewd conduct

INCIDENT

While on routine patrol at approximately 1:30 A.M., Los Angeles Police Department officers Teri Butterworth and Ernest Caldera observed a late-model white BMW parked in front of a young woman. After a few moments of conversation, she got into the car. The car made a turn onto a side street, parked again, and within moments its two occupants were placed under arrest, charged with lewd conduct. If convicted of this misdemeanor offense, each could face fines of $1,000 and up to a year in jail. The occupants of the car were British-born movie actor Hugh Grant and Los Angeles native Divine Marie Brown. ¶After his release from jail, Mr. Grant made a public statement saying that he "did something that was completely insane" and that "I have hurt people I love and embarrassed people I work with." He then flew to London to explain the incident to his supermodel girlfriend, Elizabeth Hurley. ¶Ms. Brown was also charged with a parole violation stemming from two prior convictions for prostitution. ¶Newspapers trumpeted Mr. Grant's indiscretion with banner headlines including "Blue Hugh," "Hugh's Sorry Now," and "Hugh-Miliated!" Photographers crowded around the gate of Mr. Grant and Ms. Hurley's stone cottage near Bath, England, as he and his lady love ate a tense meal in the backyard. Divine Brown reportedly sold her "story" to a London tabloid for $160,000. Mr. Grant returned to America to honor his press responsibilities for his upcoming movie <u>Nine Months</u>. Drawing high ratings, Mr. Grant's television appearances helped pave the way for <u>Nine Months</u> to make massive amounts of money at the box office. ¶At trial, Mr. Grant pleaded no contest. He apologized and was reported to have placed himself at the mercy of the court. He was fined $1,180, placed on two years' probation, and ordered to undergo AIDS education. ¶Ms. Brown pleaded not guilty, claiming that they had been arrested before any crime could take place. City Attorney William Sterling stated that he would seek the maximum eighteen-month prison term for Ms. Brown. The outcome of the Brown case had not been decided at the time of this writing. However, she has embarked on a new career as an actress.

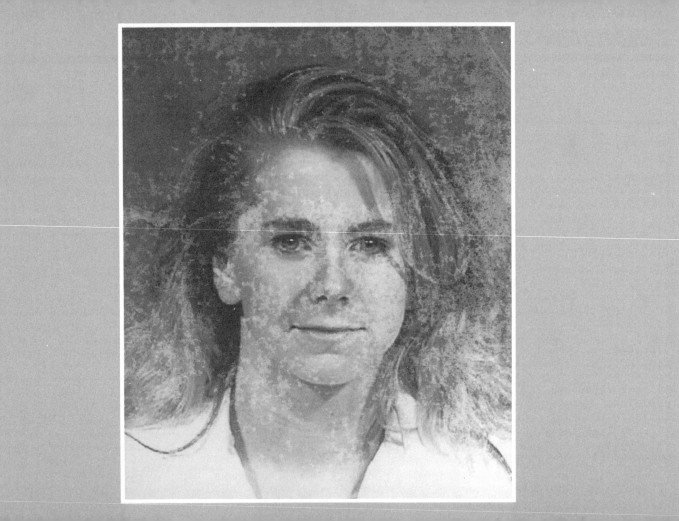

INCIDENT REPORT

NAME Tonya Harding

ARREST March 16, 1994

LOCATION Portland, Oregon

CHARGE Hindering the prosecution

INCIDENT

On December 28, 1993, while finishing her warm-up at the U.S. championships, figure skater Nancy Kerrigan was headed off the ice when a large man stepped onto the rink and clubbed her in the leg with a pipe. Kerrigan became unable to compete and Tonya Harding became U.S. champion. American television viewers watched as Kerrigan lay on the floor of the stadium shrieking in pain. The police, with the help of videotaped footage, tracked the so-called "Club Man" and identified him as Shawn Eckhart. This discovery led them to Harding's estranged husband, Jeff Gillooly. The lengthy investigation traveled to the 1994 Winter Olympics, in Norway, where the Olympic Committee debated until the last minute whether or not Ms. Harding, still the U.S. champion, was involved in the attack. Had they found that she was, she would not be allowed to compete. The Olympic Committee finally decided that it did not have enough evidence to prohibit Ms. Harding from competing in the international event. She fell to fifteenth place in the competition, while the fully recovered Nancy Kerrigan took a silver medal. ¶After the Olympics, a Multnomah County, Oregon, grand jury passed down an indictment naming Eckhart, Shane Stant, and Derrick Smith for racketeering and conspiracy to commit second-degree assault on Kerrigan. Ms. Harding and ex-husband Gillooly struck plea bargains to avoid jail time. Ms. Harding pleaded guilty to the charge of conspiracy to hinder the prosecution, and was sentenced to three years' probation with a $100,000 fine. As part of her sentence she also donated $50,000 to the Special Olympics and paid $10,000 in court costs. Ms. Harding also performed five hundred hours of community service in addition to undergoing psychiatric evaluation and treatment. As a final provision of the sentence, Ms. Harding was required to resign from the U.S. Figure Skating Association. ¶Mr. Gillooly, who served some time in jail, changed his name and was reported to have sold Penthouse magazine an hour-long X-rated videotape of his honeymoon night with Ms. Harding for $1,000,000.

INCIDENT REPORT

NAME Woody Harrelson

LOCATION Columbus, Ohio

ARREST October 10, 1982

CHARGE Disorderly conduct

INCIDENT

One evening in early October, police were called concerning a young man whose solo dancing in the middle of the street was bringing traffic to a halt. As he stumbled and fell, two police officers walked onto the road. The officers were concerned that the youth was not only causing a traffic jam but possibly endangering his own life. After young Woody Harrelson fell to his knees in the middle of the street, he was pulled to his feet by the officers and led to a waiting police van. As he was placed in the van, one of the officers noticed the smell of alcohol on his breath. ¶When the police officers began to drive off, the back door mysteriously opened and Mr. Harrelson, laughing maniacally, jumped out of the moving police van and ran. Officers chased him and when they caught up with him, the youth punched one of the officers, knocking him to the ground. The other officer, however, succeeded in handcuffing Mr. Harrelson and taking him to jail. ¶Mr. Harrelson, who was booked for disorderly conduct, was found guilty of misdemeanor assault and resisting arrest. Because of his young age, twenty-one, and his lack of prior arrests, the court was lenient: He was fined $390 and released.

Columbus Ohio - Division of Police

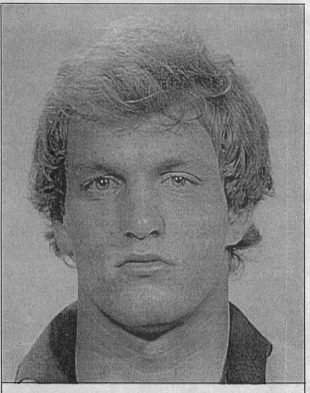

DATE OF PHOTO 06/10/93

WOODROW T. HARRELSON
45722A

AKA
AKA

SEX	**MALE**	RACE	**WHITE**
DOB	07/23/61	HEIGHT	5' 9"
WEIGHT	175	BUILD	**MEDIUM**
HAIR	**BLOND**	TEETH	**NORMAL**
FACIAL HAIR	**NONE**	SPEECH	**NORMAL**

Scars/Marks/Tatoos:

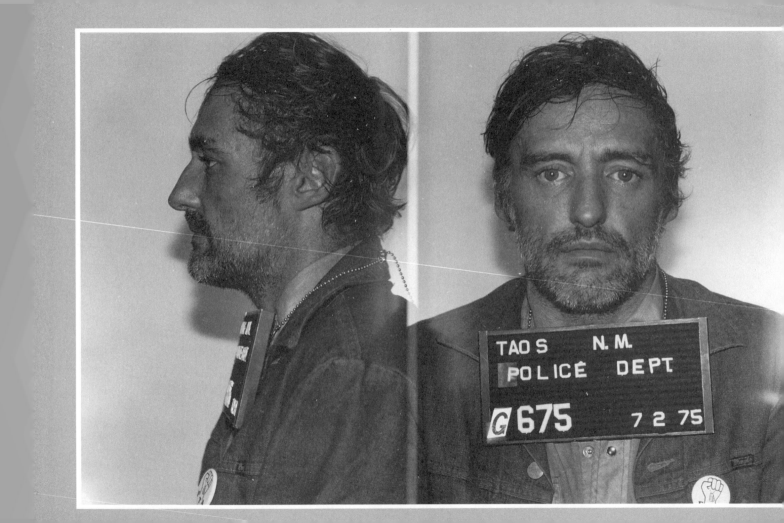

INCIDENT REPORT

NAME Dennis Hopper

ARREST July 2, 1975

LOCATION Taos, New Mexico

CHARGE Reckless driving; failure to report an accident; leaving the scene of an accident; evading police officers

INCIDENT

Identified by an eyewitness, Mr. Hopper was sought by the Taos police for a minor traffic offense and for his failure to report the incident. When Hopper could not be located, policemen requested that local Judge Montoya issue a warrant for his arrest. With warrant now in hand, officers arrested Mr. Hopper at his home. He was booked at the Taos Prisoner's Jail at 1:45 P.M. and released on a $250 bond at 2:05 P.M. ¶Five days later Mr. Hopper appeared before Judge Montoya and pleaded guilty. He was fined $250 inclusive of all charges.

INCIDENT REPORT

NAME Janis Joplin

ARREST November 16, 1967

LOCATION Tampa, Florida

CHARGE Two counts of vulgar and indecent language

INCIDENT

As a guitar intro to the Gershwin classic "Summertime" filled the Curtis-Hixon Hall in Tampa, Florida, the audience left their seats to worship near the feet of Janis Joplin. The police were edgy because of a recent near-riot in Miami involving the band The Doors, and were keeping this particular show under close scrutiny. Ms. Joplin began to sing and a growing number of fans began to block the aisles. Detective L. F. Napoli began to shout into a bull horn, instructing the audience to please return to their seats. Ms. Joplin stopped the song and remarked to the police, "I'm trying to build a sensuous mood!" She shot Detective Napoli a dirty look and the audience cheered wildly. ¶On the next song, police were again using their bull horns to urge the audience back to their seats. Ms. Joplin again addressed the police directly: "Don't fuck with those people!" Sergeant Ed Williams left the auditorium to secure a warrant for Ms. Joplin's arrest. Management then joined in the confusion by turning off the band's amplifiers and turning on the lights. These actions drove the show to a grinding halt. Ms. Joplin then lost her temper completely. After a few tense moments the show was resumed, and concluded without further incident. ¶When Ms. Joplin entered the backstage area, she found it filled with police. When she saw Detective Napoli she began a litany of curses, suddenly stopped, and walked off to her dressing room. At exactly midnight a police officer handed Ms. Joplin a warrant; she was placed under arrest and was taken to the city jail and charged with two counts of vulgar and indecent language. The first charge was based on the warrant sworn out to Sgt. Williams relating to her language during the concert. The second charge was for her language involving Detective Napoli. ¶Ms. Joplin was released following payment of a $504 bond, $252 per count. The arrest became a forum for city officials to berate the youth movement. Tampa Mayor Dick Greco stated that he would not tolerate Ms. Joplin's type of performance in his city. The trial was continued and Ms. Joplin returned to California. On March 4, 1970, she was fined $200 in absentia and the case was closed. ¶Seven months to the day afterward, Janis Joplin died of a heroin overdose.

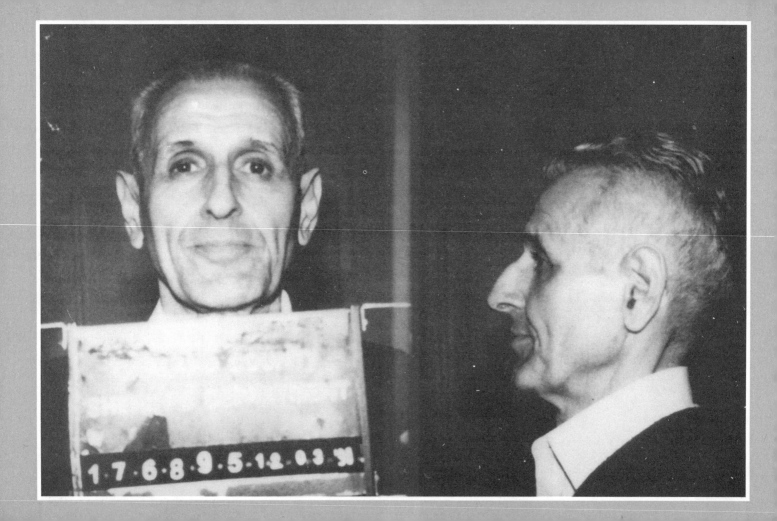

INCIDENT REPORT

NAME Jack Kevorkian

ARREST December 3, 1990

LOCATION Oakland County, Michigan

CHARGE First-degree murder

INCIDENT

Driving through a park in northern Oakland County, Michigan, retired physician Jack Kevorkian slowed his Volkswagen van to a stop. In the back lay Janet Adkins, a fifty-four-year-old former English teacher from Portland, Oregon. Ms. Adkins, suffering from Alzheimer's disease, had exhausted all traditional means of treatment. Dr. Kevorkian repaired to the back of the van and, within moments, Janet Adkins was dead. ¶Dr. Kevorkian was placed under arrest and his "suicide machine" was impounded by the Oakland County Sheriff's Office. On Friday, June 9, 1990, Dr. Kevorkian faced Oakland County Judge Alice Gilbert. He defended himself by recounting the sad tale of Janet Adkins. He had originally been contacted by Ron Adkins, the victim's husband. Mr. Adkins explained how Alzheimer's had stolen his wife's life, but said that he told her repeatedly that she need not kill herself. Ms. Adkins had explained to her husband that she was more afraid of going on than of dying. In conclusion, Kevorkian told the judge that Ms. Adkins had said, "Thank you, thank you," as she pressed the button that would subsequently end her life. By the end of the day, Judge Gilbert banned Dr. Kevorkian from assisting in any more suicides. ¶On Monday, December 3, 1990, Oakland County Prosecutor Richard Thompson subsequently charged Dr. Kevorkian with first-degree murder saying, "Dr. Kevorkian was the primary cause of Janet Adkins' death." The prosecutor added, "He can't avoid his criminal culpability by the clever use of a switch." The reference was to the doctor's suicide machine, which had been confiscated by the Oakland County Police. Dr. Kevorkian is seeking the return of his device through a civil case that began the day the murder charge was filed. ¶However, District Court Judge Gerald McNally subsequently dismissed first-degree murder charges against Dr. Kevorkian in a pretrial hearing. His decision was based on the fact that Michigan has no law against suicide or assisting a suicide, and was made after the judge listened to an audiotape of Ms. Adkins on which she discussed her fight against the disease. Ron Adkins told the press, "My family and I are very pleased and grateful to the judge for making the decision that he did." ¶As he walked out of the courtroom, Dr. Kevorkian told a reporter, "I feel like I'm walking on a cloud."

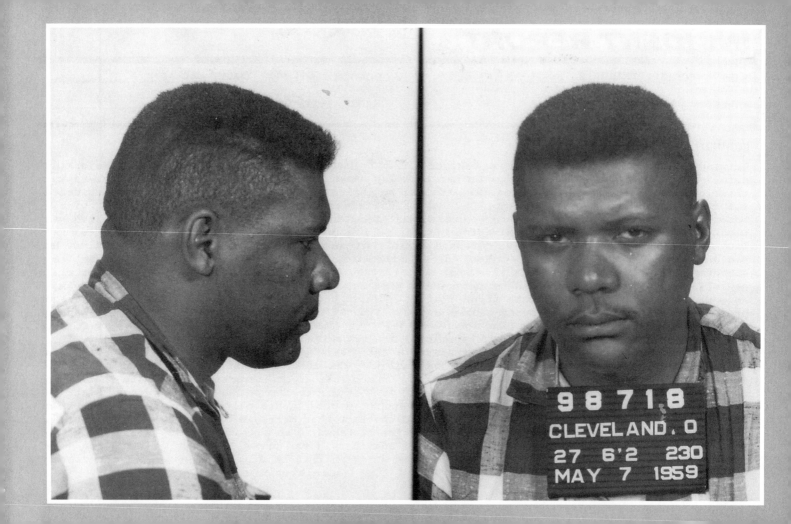

INCIDENT REPORT

NAME Don King

ARREST Cleveland, Ohio

LOCATION May 7, 1959

CHARGE Suspicion of drug dealing

INCIDENT

Between 1951 and 1967, boxing promoter Don King was a well-known criminal in and around Cleveland, Ohio. He amassed a significant number of arrests, ranging from gambling to manslaughter. In 1954, while running a gambling house, Mr. King killed Hillary Brown in what was later ruled self-defense. In 1966 Mr. King was arrested for nonnegligent manslaughter for stomping and pistol-whipping Sam Garrett to death. Garrett had failed to repay a loan made by Mr. King. Mr. King was convicted of second-degree murder, but the judge suspended the sentence and ordered a new trial, where he was found guilty of nonnegligent homicide. For this manslaughter charge, he spent three-and-a-half years in prison. In 1963, Mr. King was arrested for carrying a concealed weapon. He was the subject of several arrests and investigations from 1955 to 1963: in 1955, as a suspicious person; again in 1955, as an arsonist; in 1959, under suspicion of being a possible drug dealer; and for assault and battery in 1963. Mr. King also racked up fifteen traffic violations from 1951 to 1965, despite being known by friends and associates as a very careful driver. ¶In 1967, Mr. King was introduced on a street corner, to the fighter Cassius Clay, now known as Muhammad Ali, by singer Lloyd Price. Mr. King promoted an exhibition bout for the future champ and the rest, as they say, is history. In 1985 the Internal Revenue Service took him to court for tax evasion, but King was acquitted. Also charged was his assistant, Constance Harper, who served four months in federal prison. In 1994, the Justice Department indicted Mr. King on charges of insurance and tax fraud. The trial ended in a mistrial.

INCIDENT REPORT

NAME Larry King

ARREST December 20, 1971

LOCATION Miami, Florida

CHARGE Grand larceny

INCIDENT

From the mid-1960s until late 1971, Miami radio and television personality Larry King lived the good life. Too good: he lived far above his means. He gambled at the Hialeah Race Track, amassing a personal debt of several hundred thousand dollars. To maintain his lifestyle, King borrowed incessantly, often using his local celebrity status to borrow from banks and individuals. To help control his escalating debts, Mr. King started writing bad checks. ¶Mr. King cultivated the friendship of millionaire financier Louis Wolfson, who persuaded Mr. King to contact President-elect Richard Nixon through their mutual friend Bebe Rebozo. Mr. King asked Mr. Nixon's help in clearing Mr. Wolfson of federal charges. Mr. Nixon chose not to help and Wolfson was sent to Elgin Air Force Base, a "country club" prison in the Florida Panhandle. Upon his release, Mr. Wolfson pressed grand larceny charges against Mr. King. This was in connection with Mr. Wolfson's financial backing of New Orleans District Attorney Jim Garrison's unofficial investigation into the Kennedy assassination. According to Mr. King, who was acting as go-between, he was unable to contact Mr. Garrison to give him the $5,000 that Mr. Wolfson had sent. Mr. King then asked Mr. Wolfson if he could borrow the money himself and pay it back at a later date. Mr. King never did. ¶The trial was to begin in January 1972. Unfortunately, while reading the case brief, Judge Dan Satin suffered a heart attack and the trial was postponed. The newspapers jumped on the incident with a blaring headlines such as "Judge Collapses Reading King Brief." ¶Citing the statute of limitations, on March 10, 1972, Judge Satin dismissed the grand larceny charge. The other complainants followed suit by dropping their charges. Larry King was released. He was also released from his television and radio responsibilities and spent nearly four years off the air before returning triumphantly to Miami in 1974.

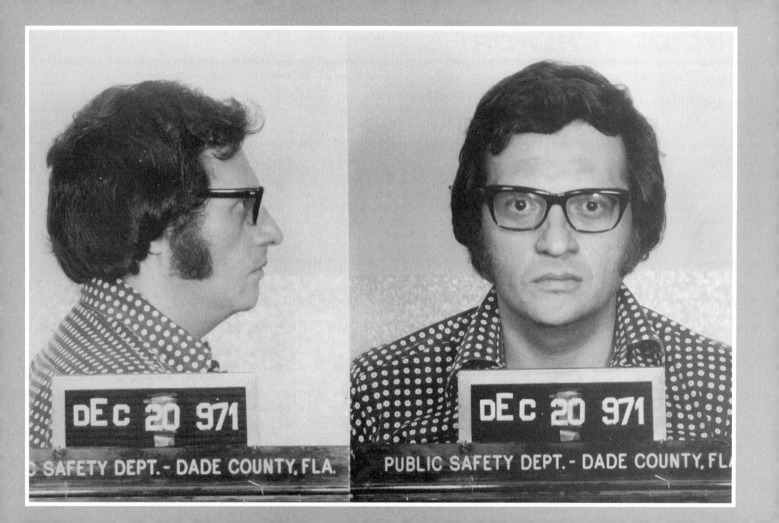

INCIDENT REPORT

NAME Evel Knievel

LOCATION Sunnyvale, California

ARREST October 10, 1994

CHARGE Corporal punishment on a cohabitant (later changed to weapon possession by an ex-felon)

INCIDENT

On the night of October 9, 1994, police responded to a call from the Comfort Inn of Santa Clara, California. According to police reports, the night clerk met the officers at the front desk and explained that there had been a loud argument in Mr. Knievel's room. Mr. Knievel had recently called to ask if the clerk would send someone to his room to get his diabetes medication and bring it to him. Wanting to avoid any trouble, the night clerk called the police to escort him. Once they arrived at the room, the clerk knocked on the door. After a brief investigation of the room, they found Mr. Knievel's girlfriend, Krystal Kennedy, aged twenty-five, in the whirlpool bath. Police noticed injuries on her face and neck. After their arrival, Mr. Knievel then called the room and the clerk answered explaining to Mr. Knievel that the police wanted to see him. ¶Two police cars were dispatched to the Brass Rail, a topless go-go bar. Mr. Knievel was arrested there at his table without incident. He was taken to the Santa Clara County Jail House and booked on charges of corporal punishment on a cohabitant. Mr. Knievel's 1984 Aston Martin was impounded by the police. During a routine inventory of the car, police discovered five weapons: a .44-caliber Magnum with a laser sight and two full clips of ammunition, a loaded .38-caliber police special, a stun gun, and two knives, one of which was double-edged and five inches long. Under the California penal code, law officers are allowed to take into custody firearms and weapons from a domestic violence case. At the arraignment, Ms. Kennedy refused to press charges, claiming that she instigated the altercation. ¶Supervising Deputy District Attorney Margo Smith made a statement that her office would not seek prosecution of Mr. Knievel on the corporal punishment charge, but would instead seek to prosecute him on a charge of weapons possession by an ex-felon. Mr. Knievel had served a six-month prison term in 1977 for beating a former TV executive with a baseball bat. Knievel claimed that he carried a concealed weapons license issued by a Montana judge. "Unfortunately for Mr. Knievel," stated Ms. Smith, "California isn't Montana." ¶Evel Knievel, the King of the Stunt Men, was released on a $10,000 bond. A trial date still has not been set as of this writing.

Name: KNIEVEL
      ROBERT

PFM #:   DJP058
CEM #:   9440624
Sex: M - MALE
Race: W - WHITE
Height: 600
Weight: 180
Birthdate: 10/17/38

          TFP Inc.

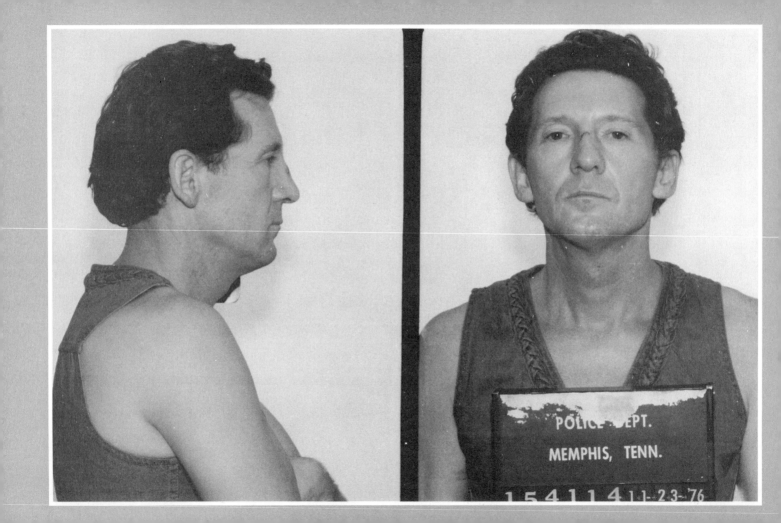

INCIDENT REPORT

NAME Jerry Lee Lewis

ARREST November 23, 1976

LOCATION Memphis, Tennessee

CHARGE Public drunkenness; carrying a pistol

INCIDENT

Robert H. Lloyd, a night guard at Graceland, called the police complaining of a drunk, pistol-wielding man blocking the gates at Elvis Presley's home in a brand-new white Lincoln Continental. Two police cars arrived at the scene at 2:56 A.M. to find Mr. Lloyd hiding in the gate house. He complained that the man in the car threatened him and told him he was going to "get in, one way or another." Mr. Lloyd had noticed that the man carried a gun in his right hand. ¶Police approached the car cautiously. The Lincoln's sole occupant sat staring out the front window. When the police got to the open driver's-side window, they found that the man was musician Jerry Lee Lewis, "The Killer." Balanced on his knee was a chrome-plated, over-under style, .38-caliber derringer pistol. Mr. Lewis was helped from his car and the gun was confiscated by the police. The officers noticed that Mr. Lewis was extremely unstable on his feet, his speech was slurred, and his breath smelled of alcohol. Mr. Lewis was apprised of his rights and was arrested for carrying a pistol and being drunk in a public place.

INCIDENT REPORT

NAME Dudley Moore

ARREST March 21, 1994

LOCATION Marina Del Rey, California

CHARGE Suspicion of domestic violence on a cohabitant

INCIDENT

Los Angeles was hushed in anticipation on the night of Monday, March 21, 1994. It was the one night of the year when Hollywood focused all of its attentions on one event, the Academy Awards. The diminutive, then fifty-nine-year-old Oscar nominee from 1981, Dudley Moore, and his girlfriend, Nicole Richardson, aged thirty, decided to spend the night at home. Some time in the middle of the evening, Mr. Moore called the police complaining about an uncontrollable domestic disturbance in his home. Moments later, Richardson called the police as well. ¶Three police cars arrived at Mr. Moore's beach-front mansion. Entering the house, officers reported observing red marks around Ms. Richardson's neck. Mr. Moore was taken into custody under suspicion of domestic violence. He was arrested under a California law designed to protect battered spouses who may not want to report their beatings for fear of reprisal. Under this statute, police are required to arrest the alleged aggressor whether the victim wants them to or not. Mr. Moore was subsequently released from jail after posting $50,000 bail. ¶Charges were dropped when Ms. Richardson requested that the district attorney's office not pursue the case. Less than three weeks later the couple were married at a private ceremony at Mr. Moore's home. About the incident, Mr. Moore stated, "I can be very difficult to live with, I get in great funks, I can't live with anyone and they can't live with me. But," he added happily, "we're working that out."

INCIDENT REPORT

NAME Eugene "Mercury" Morris

ARREST August 18, 1982

LOCATION Miami, Florida

CHARGE Three counts of selling cocaine; three counts of possessing cocaine; one count of trafficking in cocaine; one count of conspiracy to sell cocaine; one count of possession of marijuana

INCIDENT

When Florida Department of Law Enforcement undercover agent Joe Brinson knocked on the door of former Miami Dolphins football star Eugene "Mercury" Morris, the star himself opened it and led Agent Brinson into his home. As they crossed the living room, Brinson noticed large flowering marijuana plants growing all over the house. Mr. Morris and his partner, Edgar Kulins, sat down at the kitchen table with the agent. Mr. Morris then presented Brinson with 478 grams of cocaine. The ex-athlete and Mr. Kulins were arrested on drug charges and taken into custody. ¶At their arraignment, Mr. Kulins pleaded guilty while Mr. Morris maintained his innocence. His trial, before Circuit Judge Ellen Morphonius Gable, received enormous local media attention. Mr. Morris, a three-time All-Pro who had been part of the legendary 1972 Dolphins team, was facing up to one hundred years in prison. Mr. Morris maintained his innocence throughout the proceedings, even in the face of audiotaped evidence on which he was heard planning the drug deal. ¶Judge Gable found Mr. Morris guilty of trafficking cocaine, a conviction that under Florida's "get-tough" drug laws carried a minimum of fifteen years in prison without parole. She sentenced the running back to twenty years and fined him $250,000. ¶Mr. Morris appealed his conviction twice to no avail. On his third attempt he was granted a new trial by the Florida Supreme Court. On June 12, 1986, after serving three and a half years in prison, he again faced Judge Gable, and changed his plea to no contest, this time to a cocaine conspiracy charge, in exchange for his freedom. (Under the new charge, Mr. Morris was ordered to serve four and a half years, but having already served most of that time and having remained on good behavior, he was not required to return to prison.) While incarcerated Mr. Morris decided to dedicate his life to saving the youth of south Florida from the ills of drug abuse. He has since brought this message to thousands of people by lecturing across the country and writing a book about his experience, entitled <u>Against the Grain</u>.

INCIDENT REPORT

NAME Jim Morrison

ARREST December 9, 1967

LOCATION New Haven, Connecticut

CHARGE Breach of peace; resisting arrest; immoral exhibition

INCIDENT

It was Jim Morrison's twenty-fourth birthday. His band, The Doors, was playing at Troy, New York's Rensselaer Polytechnic Institute's field house. The audience was underwhelmed by these satyrlike upstarts from California. The band was touring to promote two hit records that had been released earlier that year, and yet hadn't even earned an encore in Troy. Disappointed and depressed, the band piled into a limousine and drove the four-hour trip to New Haven, Connecticut. ¶Rumors about The Doors's penchant for trouble—and the lustful interest of their young female fans—made the police want to keep the band as far away from the general population as possible. ¶On a routine pre-concert check, a police officer found a couple engaged in amorous activity in a shower stall. When he told the couple to leave, the male—Mr. Morrison—became belligerent. The altercation ended when the police officer sprayed the young man with mace. Screaming in pain, Mr. Morrison ran into the dressing room. The police were now hot on his trail. As the officers entered the dressing room, they were met by the band's manager, Bill Siddons, who pleaded with them not to take the singer into custody. The police assented and soon the recovered Jim Morrison and The Doors took the stage to an enthusiastic reception. ¶On stage, The Doors thrilled the crowd to a legendary performance. While performing their song "Back Door Man," the last number of the evening, Mr. Morrison began to tell the audience about what had happened backstage, using a mocking, Southern drawl. As he spoke, the audience began to get loud and restless. As he ended the story he began screaming, "The whole world hates me, the whole world fucking hates me!" He then returned to the song as if he had never stopped singing. ¶Police then turned on the auditorium lights, rushed the stage, and arrested Mr. Morrison. The band stopped playing, and Mr. Morrison was dragged off the stage. The police informed the audience that the show was over. Fearing a riot, police began arresting people. Many of those arrested were members of the press. At the Court Street station, Mr. Morrison was booked for "breach of peace, resisting arrest, and immoral exhibition," and later released on a $1,500 bail bond. ¶A few weeks later most of the charges were dropped. Mr. Morrison was fined $25 for breach of peace, but the district attorney's office decided not to pursue the other two charges.

INCIDENT REPORT

NAME Bess Myerson

ARREST October 21, 1987

LOCATION New York, New York

CHARGE Bribery; conspiracy; mail fraud; and obstruction of justice

INCIDENT

When Bess Myerson entered the Federal Courthouse in downtown New York City she looked like a beauty queen. Under her Chanel suit and Hermès scarf, she wore a scarlet blouse. Beside her stood her boyfriend, Carl (Andy) Capasso, eighteen years her junior. He had just arrived under police escort from the federal prison in Allenwood, Pennsylvania, where he was serving a four-year sentence for tax fraud. ¶The occasion: Rudolph Giuliani, then U.S. attorney, announced Ms. Myerson's indictment, which accused her of conspiring with State Supreme Court Justice Hortense Gabel to reduce Mr. Capasso's alimony payments. The indictment further stated that Judge Gabel entered into this conspiracy in exchange for a job for her daughter Sukhreet, who had been hired by Ms. Myerson to work for the New York City Cultural Affairs Commission, which Ms. Myerson then headed. ¶Three months after Judge Gabel reduced Andy Capasso's alimony by two-thirds (to $60,000 a year), Sukhreet Gabel was fired by the Cultural Affairs Commission. The young Gabel then decided to go to the U.S. Attorney. She assisted the U.S. Attorney's office by providing documents from her mother's office, and secretly recording phone conversations with her mother, evidence which led to the indictment. The action forced Judge Gabel to resign from the bench. ¶Fortunately for Ms. Myerson, the evidence did not hold in Federal Court. Her lawyer told the jury that the prosecutor's attempts to establish guilt "would have gotten them hauled off 'The Gong Show'!" and on December 23, 1988, after nearly five days of deliberations, the jury found Ms. Myerson, Mr. Capasso, and Judge Gabel not guilty of a divorce-fixing conspiracy. Cheers arose in the courtroom as the acquittals were handed down. The jury forewoman later stated that "given the prosecution's case, I had no other choice but to say not guilty."

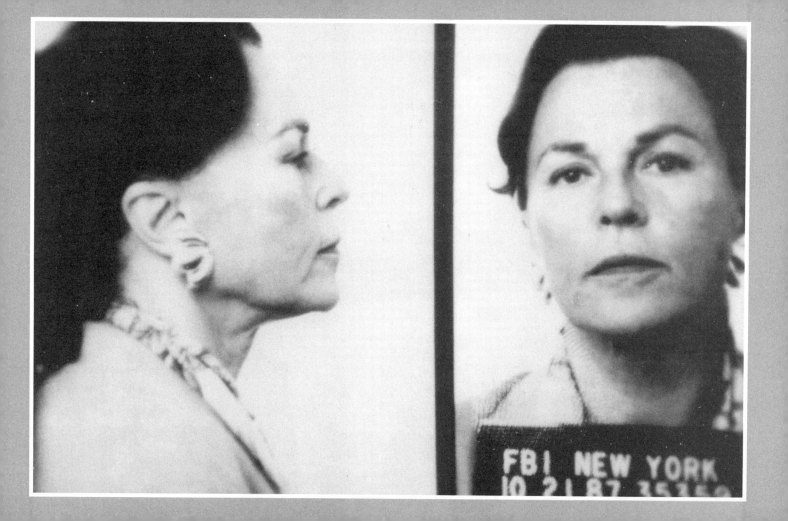

FBI NEW YORK
10 21 87 35358

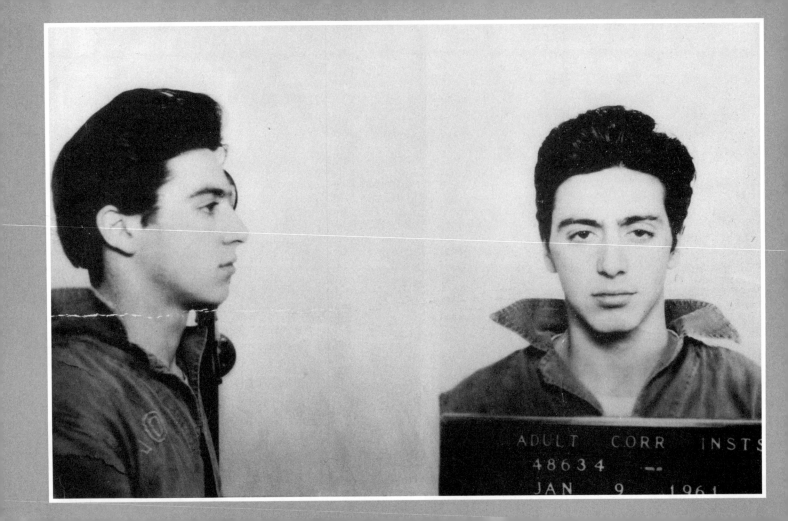

ADULT CORR INSTS
48634 --
JAN 9 1961

INCIDENT REPORT

NAME Al Pacino

ARREST January 7, 1961

LOCATION Woonsocket, Rhode Island

CHARGE Carrying a concealed weapon

INCIDENT

Two policemen sat in their parked squad car on Park Avenue, in a suburb of Providence, Rhode Island. It was well into the graveyard shift, when the officers noticed that the same car had passed them several times. Officer William J. O'Coin, Jr., decided that they should pull the suspicious vehicle over. O'Coin approached the car with his flashlight on and looked in the car. He noticed that the three occupants were wearing black masks and gloves. "Don't tell me," the officer asked sarcastically, "you're coming from a Halloween party." ¶The police officers had the men get out of the car. The driver was Vincent J. Calcagni, of Rhode Island, his two passengers were nineteen-year-old Bruce Cohen and twenty-year-old Alphonse Pacino, both from New York City. A search of the car's trunk turned up a loaded .38 caliber pistol. The three men were then taken to the police station and booked. ¶During the interviews, William J. O'Coin remembered that Mr. Pacino had been very helpful. He explained that they were all actors and that he and Mr. Cohen had taken the bus up from New York to visit Mr. Calcagni, whom he had met in the service. The young men were not able to pay the $2,000 bail and were all sent to jail. The reported duration of Mr. Pacino's stay behind bars was three days. There is no record of whether he or the others were ever prosecuted or convicted.

INCIDENT REPORT

NAME Joe Pepitone

ARREST March 18, 1985

LOCATION Brooklyn, New York

CHARGE Two counts of possession of a controlled substance; one count of criminal possession of a weapon; one count of use of drug paraphernalia

INCIDENT

At 10:30 P.M., police pulled over a late-model sedan for running a red light in the Brownsville section of Brooklyn. As the officers approached the vehicle they noticed three men inside. On the front seat between the driver and the passenger's seat was a clear plastic bag filled with pills. A thorough search of the car and its occupants turned up almost ten ounces of cocaine, a small quantity of heroin, various drug paraphernalia, glassine envelopes, records of drug transactions, and a loaded gun. Further investigation identified the pills as Quaaludes and the driver of the car as former star Yankee Joe Pepitone. ¶At his trial for drug and weapons charges, Joe Pep's attorney, John Q. Kelly, successfully argued that his client was not guilty of the felony charges. In New York, conviction could have brought him a life sentence. The lawyer was not as lucky with the two misdemeanor counts: Mr. Pepitone was found guilty of possession of Quaaludes and possession of drug paraphernalia. Each misdemeanor charge carried a year sentence; Kelly was able to get the prison time reduced to six months and immediately filed an appeal. ¶At Mr. Pepitone's sentencing, Brooklyn Supreme Court Justice Allan Marrus described Pepitone as the "former Bronx Bomber" who was now "just a very ordinary Brooklyn criminal." The judge was also quoted as saying, "I find it particularly sad that someone who wore Yankee pinstripes would now be wearing prison stripes." After Mr. Pepitone's appeal on May 17, 1988, was denied, he was remanded to New York's Riker's Island Detention Center to serve his six-month term.

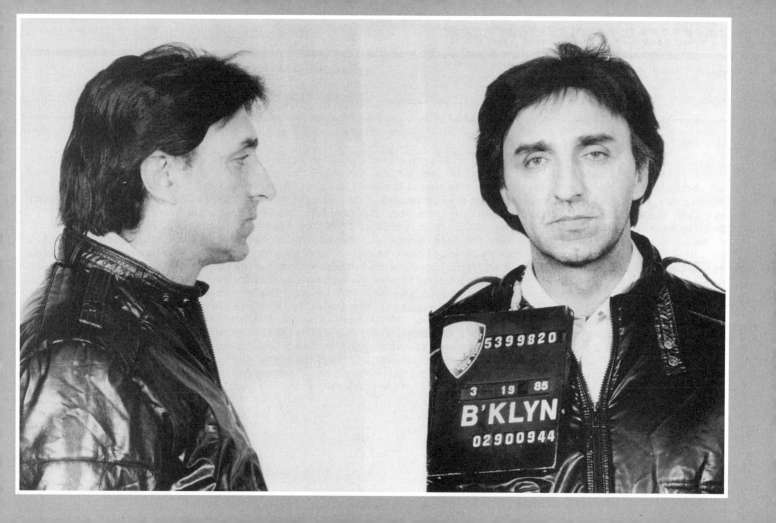

INCIDENT REPORT

NAME Dana Plato

LOCATION Las Vegas, Nevada

ARREST January 21, 1992

CHARGE Armed robbery

INCIDENT

Wearing a black hat and wraparound sunglasses, Dana Plato, a former child star, entered her local video store. Pulling out what appeared to be an automatic pistol, she approached the clerk and demanded, "Give me your money." The cashier, Heather Dailey, complied and Ms. Plato ran out of the store. Ms. Plato, who played Kimberly Drummond, the daughter of a billionaire, on television, escaped with $164 in cash. Ms. Dailey picked up the phone, dialed 9-1-1 and told the police, "I've just been robbed by Kimberly from 'Diff'rent Strokes'!" ¶When Las Vegas police arrived at the scene, a small crowd had gathered at the store's entrance. Among the crowd was Ms. Plato, acting like all of the other rubber-neckers. Ms. Dailey pointed her out, and she was immediately taken into custody. Searching her apartment, Police Officer Charles Davidiatis found a pellet gun that looked like the handgun used in the alleged robbery. Ms. Plato was subsequently taken to the Clark County Detention Center, where she remained until she posted the $13,000 bail. (The money supposedly came from selling her story to the tabloid newspaper The Star.) She received five years' probation and was ordered to do two hundred hours of community service. ¶Some have suggested Ms. Plato contrived the ill-fated heist as a publicity stunt to revive her flagging career after "Diff'rent Strokes." She had moved to Las Vegas to look for work and, after losing her job as a counter girl at a dry cleaner, appeared in Playboy magazine. She maintained that she had robbed the store not for attention but, as she stated in The Star, "to pay the rent." At her arraignment, Ms. Plato pleaded innocent. Ultimately, Ms. Plato pleaded guilty to a reduced charge of attempted robbery.

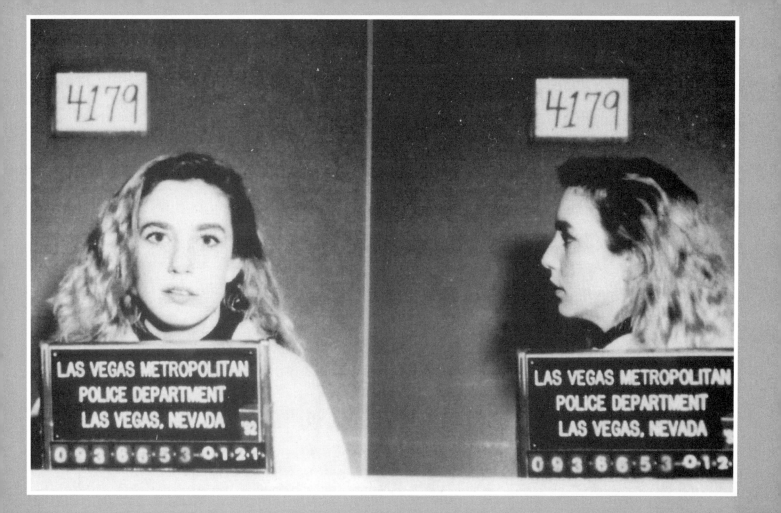

INCIDENT REPORT

NAME Keanu Reeves

ARREST May 5, 1993

LOCATION Los Angeles, California

CHARGE Drunk driving

INCIDENT

According to several reports, the <u>Speed</u> star was pulled over late one night for driving erratically. He was booked on a DUI charge and released on his own recognizance. According to published sources, it was this mug shot that supposedly "straightened out" the young star. It is said that, upon seeing his photo, Mr. Reeves was reminded of his own father, Samuel Reeves, who is currently serving a ten-year prison sentence on drug charges.

INCIDENT REPORT

NAME Paul Reubens (Pee-wee Herman)

ARREST July 26, 1991

LOCATION Sarasota, Florida

CHARGE Indecent exposure

INCIDENT

On July 26, 1991, Paul Reubens—also known as Pee-wee Herman, star of "Pee-wee's Playhouse," the most successful children's television show since "Howdy Doody"—was arrested for exposing himself inside the South Trail Cinema, an adult theater. During a showing of <u>Nancy Nurse Turns Up the Heat</u>, the actor was allegedly observed exposing himself by two undercover detectives. Along with Mr. Reubens, three other men were arrested. Lieutenant Bill Stoolkey, a Sarasota County sheriff, stated that if convicted Mr. Reubens could face sixty days in prison and a $500 fine, and that the actor had identified himself as Pee-wee Herman. The performer's lawyer, Dan Dannheiser, was mystified by his famous client's need to tell the police who he was. ¶At the courthouse on Ringling Boulevard, Mr. Reubens avoided a media circus by pleading no contest to the indecent exposure charges. Judge Judy Goldman of Sarasota County stated that prosecutors and Mr. Reubens could forego a trial in exchange for that plea, which included a $50 fine and a promise of seventy-five hours of community service. Mr. Reubens's plea agreement included an antidrug videotape to be made available to schools and local television stations, which Mr. Reubens agreed to write, produce, and fund himself. He also had to pay the $85.75 court costs. Judge Goldman noted that the small fines were "not a proper measure" and stated that she would later impose harsher penalties if Mr. Reubens failed to meet the other terms of the agreement. ¶Mr. Reubens—once known as a lovable star of children's television—has since had all records of his trial sealed by the court. His career plummeted after his arrest. CBS immediately canceled "Pee-wee's Playhouse," and his magazine, toys, and line of children's books were pulled from store shelves during the fallout. "Due to this horrible injustice," said lawyer Dan Dannheiser, "Paul has lost everything." ¶Today, these once-popular Pee-wee toys are extremely rare and much sought after by toy collectors. Paul Reubens has had bit parts in several movies, including <u>Batman Returns</u> and <u>Buffy the Vampire Slayer</u>, and appeared on the popular TV show "Murphy Brown." ¶The Sarasota police procedure of visiting pornographic theaters was questioned after a public outcry that it is a waste of manpower and a distortion of priorities.

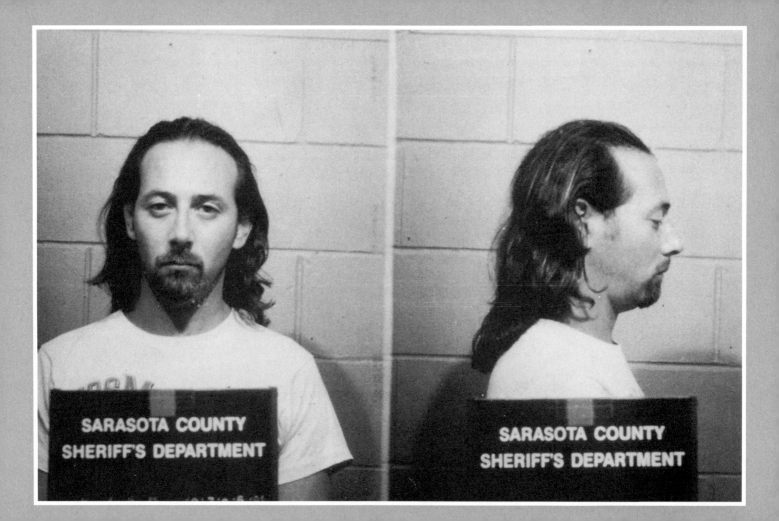

SARASOTA COUNTY
SHERIFF'S DEPARTMENT

SARASOTA COUNTY
SHERIFF'S DEPARTMENT

INCIDENT REPORT

NAME   Eric Roberts

ARREST   February 8, 1995

LOCATION   Los Angeles, California

CHARGE   Investigation of spousal abuse

INCIDENT

The actor Eric Roberts, older brother of actress Julia Roberts, was arrested after allegedly shoving his wife, Eliza Garrett, into a wall. He was picked up by police at approximately 5:00 A.M., and released around midnight after posting a $50,000 bail. ¶At this writing, the Los Angeles district attorney had not decided whether or not to pursue an indictment against the actor.

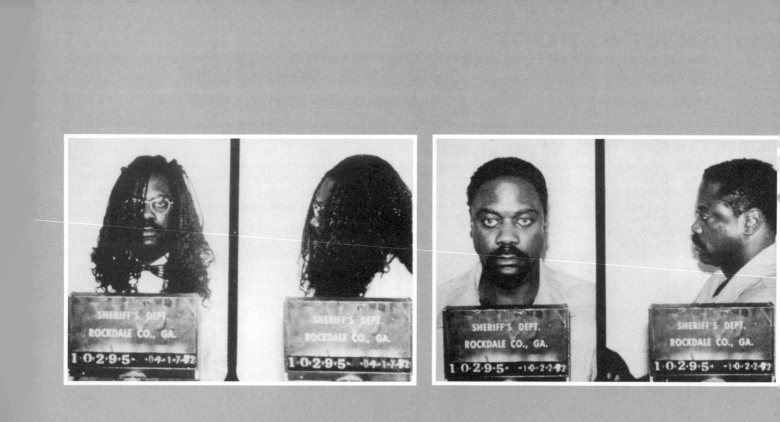

INCIDENT REPORT

NAME Howard Rollins

ARREST January 19, 1993

LOCATION Rockdale County, Georgia

CHARGE Driving under the influence; driving with a suspended license; speeding; violating parole; reckless driving

INCIDENT

On January 19, 1993, for the fourth time in eighteen months, Howard Rollins, Academy Award nominee and star of the hit television series, "In the Heat of the Night," was arrested for speeding and driving without a license. He was mistakenly released on the following day, and a warrant was issued for his arrest for probation violation. Later, on March 26, 1993, another warrant came down for failure to appear in court. As a fugitive in Georgia with two outstanding warrants, Rollins faced up to six months in prison. ¶Mr. Rollins's first arrest was on May 1, 1992, on charges of driving his maroon Nissan 300ZX while under the influence of a prescription drug, reckless driving, and failure to maintain a lane while driving through an intersection. He was fined $1,153, sentenced to ten days in jail (subsequently suspended), and paroled with twelve months probation, license suspension, and an order to undergo weekly drug screenings. On September 17, he was arrested for DUI again. This time, he was wearing a disguise, of a braided wig and eyeglasses. His parole was revoked on October 7, when he failed to submit to his weekly drug screenings. Mr. Rollins was next arrested in Newton County, Georgia, on October 17, for driving under the influence, speeding, and driving with a suspended license. He was fined $1,105. ¶On October 22, Mr. Rollins reported to the Rockdale County Jail, where he served forty-seven days of a ninety-day sentence. He was then remanded to the Dekalb Diversion Center, where he became part of the Chances drug-rehabilitation program. On January 19, 1993, Mr. Rollins was arrested for speeding and driving without a license and the two warrants were subsequently issued. ¶On May 10, Sheriff Guy Norman made a statement to reporters that the actor, Howard Rollins, had turned himself in to the Rockdale County Jail, after having been a fugitive for several months. Mr. Rollins requested solitary confinement during his prison stay. ¶On November 4, after completing a ten-week prison term, Mr. Rollins returned to the set of "In the Heat of the Night." Two days later, he was arrested on Iris Drive in Conyers, Georgia. His automobile was pulled over for weaving and the former Oscar nominee failed a roadside sobriety test. He was arrested and booked for drunk driving and several other traffic-related charges.

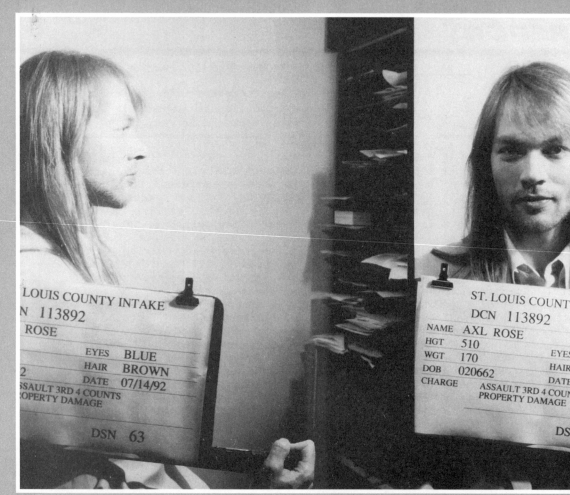

ST. LOUIS COUNTY INTAKE

DCN 113892

NAME	AXL ROSE
HGT	510
WGT	170
DOB	020662
CHARGE	

EYES	BLUE
HAIR	BROWN
DATE	07/14/92

ASSAULT 3RD 4 COUNTS
PROPERTY DAMAGE

DSN 63

INCIDENT REPORT

INCIDENT

Riverport Amphitheater was packed to capacity for a performance by the popular heavy-metal rock group Guns N' Roses that hot July night in St. Louis. Approximately ninety minutes into the show, lead singer Axl Rose began to point into the audience. "Take that, take that!" he shouted to the security guards. "Get that guy and take that!" The befuddled security guards began to scan the crowd. The guards knew the problem was a camera, one of Mr. Rose's pet peeves, but they couldn't see it from the theater's floor. ¶Mr. Rose screamed into the microphone, "If security isn't going to do anything about it, then I will!" He leaped off the stage and dove into the audience. He landed on William "Stump" Stephenson, a member of the Saddle Tramps Motorcycle Club. After a brief scuffle, Mr. Rose returned to the stage and announced, "Thanks to the...security, I'm going home!" He then threw down his microphone and stalked off the stage. After a moment of confusion, the band followed. Within moments, a riot broke out. ¶Bottles and debris were thrown at the stage as approximately three thousand of the estimated fifteen thousand concert-goers took part in the melee. Sixty-five people were injured and considerable damage was done to the amphitheater. ¶Local officials wanting to curb the rise of rock-related violence arranged for a warrant to be issued for Mr. Rose's arrest. Police searched for the singer, but Guns N' Roses was on a world tour and had already left the city. ¶On July 17, 1992, Mr. Rose was arrested at New York's John F. Kennedy International Airport by U.S. Customs officials as he returned to the United States after completing the European leg of Guns N' Roses's world tour. He was taken into custody and pleaded not guilty at his arraignment in St. Louis. Mr. Rose was convicted of four counts of misdemeanor assault and one count of property damage. He was fined and put on two years' probation.

INCIDENT REPORT

NAME   Mickey Rourke

ARREST   July 18, 1994

LOCATION   Los Angeles, California

CHARGE   Spousal abuse

INCIDENT

Actor-boxer Mickey Rourke and the model-actress Carre Otis met while making an X-rated film called Wild Orchid. Their on-screen electricity led to a romance and then marriage. Five months later, Ms. Otis was hospitalized for depression. In 1991, while on location with Mr. Rourke, Ms. Otis was rushed to a New Mexico hospital with a bullet wound in her shoulder. She told police that her husband didn't shoot her, explaining that she had moved a bag that contained a .357 Magnum and it accidentally went off. ¶On July 18, 1994, the Los Angeles Police Department arrested Mr. Rourke for allegedly slapping and kicking Ms. Otis. He pleaded innocent to the charges. The couple then separated and later divorced. On December 12, a California judge dismissed the spousal abuse charges against Mr. Rourke after Ms. Otis stopped cooperating with the Los Angeles prosecutors. ¶Early in 1995, during Fashion Week in New York City, a yearly event for the fashion industry, Ms. Otis attempted to relaunch her modeling career. Rumors, thought to have been spread by Ms. Otis, began to circulate: her ex-husband was said to be stalking her. This got Mr. Rourke banned from many of the fashion show's events. The former couple's close encounters at the shows and at parties made front-page headlines, upstaging even the designers. For example, at one party Mr. Rourke sent rapper Tupac Shakur, who was himself on trial for sexual assault, to Ms. Otis's table with a bottle of champagne. ¶In mid-1995 Ms. Otis moved back in with Mr. Rourke. In her own words, Ms. Otis stated that "we are very, very happy."

INCIDENT REPORT

NAME Orenthal James (O. J.) Simpson

LOCATION Los Angeles, California

ARREST June 17, 1994

CHARGE Two counts of murder in the first degree

INCIDENT

In the early morning of June 13, 1994, police were summoned to a home on Bundy Drive in the Brentwood section of Los Angeles. There they found two horribly wounded corpses, Nicole Brown Simpson and Ronald Goldman. In the house were Ms. Simpson's two children asleep in their rooms. Police contacted Mr. Simpson, who was on a business trip to Chicago, and informed him that his ex-wife and a man had been killed. Mr. Simpson returned to Los Angeles. Within a day, he realized that the investigation had begun to revolve around him. He was requested to surrender himself to the Los Angeles Police Department; instead of complying, he surreptitiously left the house of a lawyer friend in a white Ford Bronco. The whole country watched on television as he and his friend, A. C. Cowlings, were chased, albeit at a stately pace, along a Los Angeles freeway. Mr. Simpson was eventually placed under arrest and charged with the two murders. ¶Over the next year America and the world would be held in the grip of what the media would dub the "Trial of the Century." Mr. Simpson hired what some have called the finest legal team ever assembled, led by Johnnie Cochran, who had never lost a case in Los Angeles, and criminal defense attorney Robert Shapiro. In their defense lineup, they brought out a virtual Who's Who of law, including legendary trial lawyer F. Lee Bailey, constitutional law expert and Harvard professor Alan Dershowitz, DNA experts Barry Scheck and Peter Neufeld, California evidence expert Bob Blaiser, former president of the California Academy of Appellate Lawyers Dean Ullman, and Simpson's friend Robert Kardashian. The "Dream Team," as they were dubbed in the press, held the prosecution's representatives, Los Angeles city attorneys Marcia Clark and Christopher Darden and their case at bay. ¶Finally, after nine months of trial, Mr. Simpson was found not guilty and released. There have been more pages written about this case than any other in history.

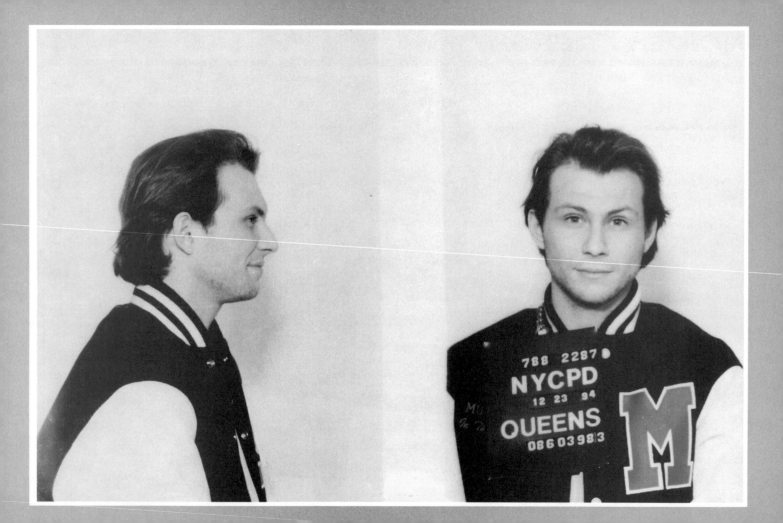

INCIDENT REPORT

NAME Christian Slater

ARREST December 23, 1994

LOCATION Queens, New York

CHARGE Criminal possession of a weapon

INCIDENT

Actor Christian Slater was planning to board a Delta flight to Los Angeles from New York's John F. Kennedy International Airport. He checked his luggage and continued on to the gate with a black nylon bag. Mr. Slater placed the bag on the conveyor belt at the metal detector, and within moments, he was placed under arrest for possession of a handgun. His bag contained a 7.65 Baretta semiautomatic pistol, criminal possession of which could carry a prison term of up to seven years. Mr. Slater was released on his own recognizance some hours later, on Christmas Eve. ¶On March 17, 1995, Mr. Slater and his attorney, Joseph DiBoasi, successfully negotiated a plea bargain with Assistant District Attorney John Larsen. The charge of criminal possession of a weapon was downgraded to a misdemeanor charge of attempted weapons possession. Slater, who owned the licensed and empty weapon, faced Queens Criminal Court Judge James Griffin, who sentenced him to three days of community service with the Children's Health Project, which provides medical care to children in homeless shelters. The Queens district attorney's Office issued this statement: "The nature of community service will do more benefit for the city than would [Slater's] incarceration."

INCIDENT REPORT

INCIDENT

The twenty-three-year-old actress and model was arrested for bouncing checks totaling about $100. She had been told that a check for modeling work was on its way, but she never received the check and did not have the funds to cover the checks she had written. ¶As was the custom of the day, she was taken into custody, booked, printed, and strip searched. In the late 1960s, San Francisco had become a magnet for young people from across the country. As a result, the police were forced to take sterner measures to help stem the tide of youth-oriented crime. ¶Ms. Somers avoided prosecution by promising to make reparations and cover the check. She eventually made good on her promise and no further action was taken.

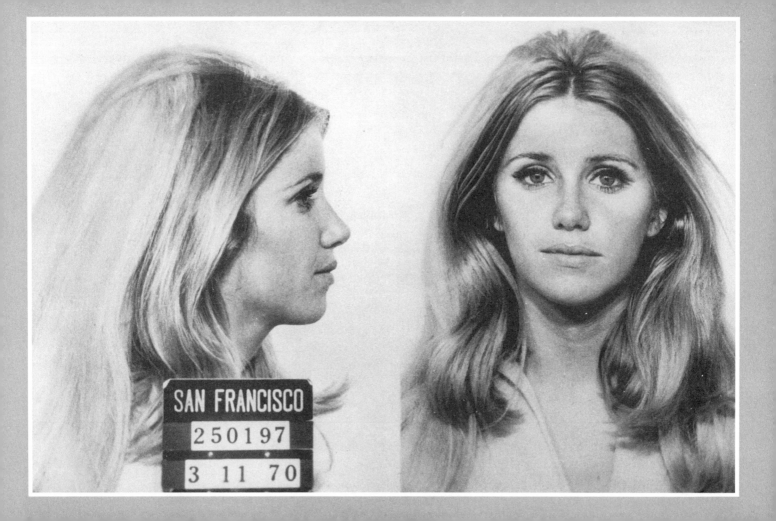

SAN FRANCISCO
250197
3 11 70

INCIDENT REPORT

NAME Mike Tyson

ARREST September 11, 1991

LOCATION Indianapolis, Indiana

CHARGE Rape

INCIDENT

On September 9, 1991, an Indianapolis grand jury indicted 1987 heavyweight champion of the world Mike Tyson on the charge of rape. The charge stemmed from an incident that occurred at the Canterbury Hotel in Indianapolis during the Miss Black America pageant, in which the boxer had been a judge. Mr. Tyson surrendered to authorities two days after the indictment was handed down. Accompanied by a lawyer from Washington, Vincent Fuller, and his local counsel, James Voyles, Mr. Tyson faced Marion County Supreme Court Judge Patricia J. Gifford. The judge read the four counts of the indictment: one count of rape, two counts of criminal deviate conduct, and one count of confinement. Mr. Tyson entered a plea of "not guilty." ¶During the thirteen-day trial much was made of the intentions of the eighteen-year-old victim, Desiree Washington, a Sunday school teacher, who was a contestant in the Miss Black America contest. The prosecution maintained that the young woman had been taken advantage of by the champion, who acted like a "wolf in sheep's clothing." ¶According to prosecutors, Mr. Tyson presented the epitome of gentlemanly behavior. He escorted Ms. Washington to many of the events at the Black Expo of which the pageant was but one feature, driving her in his car. He introduced her to several of his high-profile friends, and when they returned to the hotel, she gladly accepted his friendly invitation to go to his room. The defense attempted to paint Ms. Washington as a "shameless gold digger" who only pressed charges after she realized her encounter was a one-night stand. The defense's case was decimated by inconsistencies between Mr. Tyson's grand jury testimony and his testimony on the stand. After deliberating for nearly ten hours, the jury found Mr. Tyson guilty of the one count of rape and two counts of criminal deviate behavior. ¶At the sentencing, Mr. Tyson received a term of ten years in prison for the rape of Desiree Washington. Judge Gifford suspended four of those years, making Tyson's maximum prison stay six years. He was remanded to the Indiana Youth Center in Plainfield, Indiana. Inmate Number 922335, as Mr. Tyson became known, spent almost three years there. While there, he became a voracious reader and converted to Islam. A few days after his release, Don King, Mr. Tyson's manager, announced that Mike Tyson would fight again.

INCIDENT REPORT

NAME Sid Vicious (John Simon Ritchie) **LOCATION** New York City

ARREST October 12, 1978 **CHARGE** Second-degree murder

INCIDENT

Following the breakup of the band the Sex Pistols in January 1978, Sid Vicious, the band's erstwhile bassist, and his girlfriend, Nancy Spungen, checked into the Chelsea Hotel as Mr. and Mrs. John Simon Ritchie. In New York the two of them tried to clean up their acts and they entered a methadone program, but unfortunately supplemented their habits with various prescription drugs and the "occasional" taste of heroin. ¶On the morning of October 12, at approximately 10:50 A.M., the hotel received a call. The person suggested someone check on the occupants of room 100. "Someone is seriously injured," said the caller, "and I'm not kidding, man." Mr. Vicious returned to the hotel from a methadone clinic moments before the police arrived. Ms. Spungen, clad only in a black bra and panties, lay dead in the bathroom. The single wound in her abdomen was caused, presumably, by the blood-stained hunting knife found on the bathroom floor. ¶Mr. Vicious was taken into custody and his British passport was confiscated by the police. At his arraignment on a murder charge, he collapsed from methadone withdrawal. Revived, he was incarcerated in New York's Riker's Island Detention Center. On October 22, one day after Nancy Spungen's funeral, Mr. Vicious was released on $50,000 bail into the care of his manager, Malcolm McLaren, and his mother, Ann Beverly. When he attempted suicide that day, he was placed in Bellevue Hospital for observation. After his release, Mr. Vicious returned to Riker's Island for cutting a man with a broken bottle in a nightclub. ¶If convicted, Mr. Vicious could have faced a sentence of up to twenty-five years in prison. On February 1, 1979, he was released on bail for the second time. He had been "detoxed" and was probably in the best health he had enjoyed in years. However, when his mother met him at the courthouse, she had bought some heroin for him. At the home of a friend, he shot up for the first time in two months. His mother warned him that she'd been told the purity of the heroin was very high, but Mr. Vicious ignored the warning and almost overdosed on his second shot later that day. Sometime in the early morning of February 2, Mr. Vicious injected himself with a lethal dose of heroin. His body was discovered by his mother. Sid Vicious had died three months shy of his twenty-first birthday.

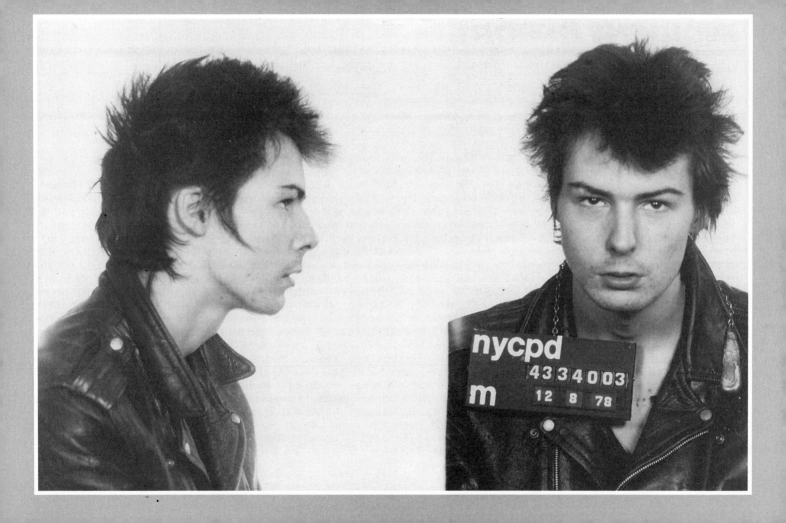

INCIDENT REPORT

NAME Wendy O. Williams

ARREST January 19, 1981

LOCATION Milwaukee, Wisconsin

CHARGE Conduct prohibited in a class B tavern; battery on a police officer; resisting arrest

INCIDENT

The hype surrounding the band The Plasmatics reached an all-time high in 1980, when lead singer Wendy O. Williams drove a Cadillac down a New York pier into an exploding wall of television sets. She leapt to safety seconds before the explosion. This action was the culmination of the band's stage show, which typically included dismantling guitars with chain saws, smashing televisions with a sledgehammer, and Ms. Williams's occasional on-stage nudity. It was these antics, as reported in the Milwaukee Sentinel, that gave the Milwaukee police the notion to attend the band's concert at the Palms Club on January 19, 1981. ¶During the concert, Ms. Williams reportedly performed not only the usual acts of destruction but was also accused of rubbing herself in a provocative manner with a sledgehammer. After the show, Ms. Williams was placed under arrest and escorted to a police van. A police officer allegedly groped her in sexually abusive manner, she slapped the officer's face and was reportedly thrown to the ground by police officers who attempted to restrain the 107-pound singer. ¶When the band's manager, Rod Swenson, tried to break up the fracas, he himself was pulled away by three officers who allegedly proceeded to sedate him with the use of their billy clubs. The unconscious Swenson was taken to a hospital and was treated for a concussion. Wendy O. Williams was handcuffed ankle and wrist and dragged to the police station. A female police officer insisted that Ms. Williams be taken to a hospital, where she received seven stitches above her left eye. Upon her return to the police station, Williams, Swenson, and the band's bassist, Jean Beauvoir (who was charged with disorderly conduct and resisting arrest), were arrested and booked. After a night in jail they were each released on separate $2,000 bonds. ¶The Plasmatics hurried to their next gig in Cleveland, Ohio. While leaving the stage, Ms. Williams collapsed and was taken to the hospital. She was treated for exhaustion and her damaged left eye. Ms. Williams left the hospital in the early morning and was placed under arrest by Cleveland police on a charge of pandering obscenities.

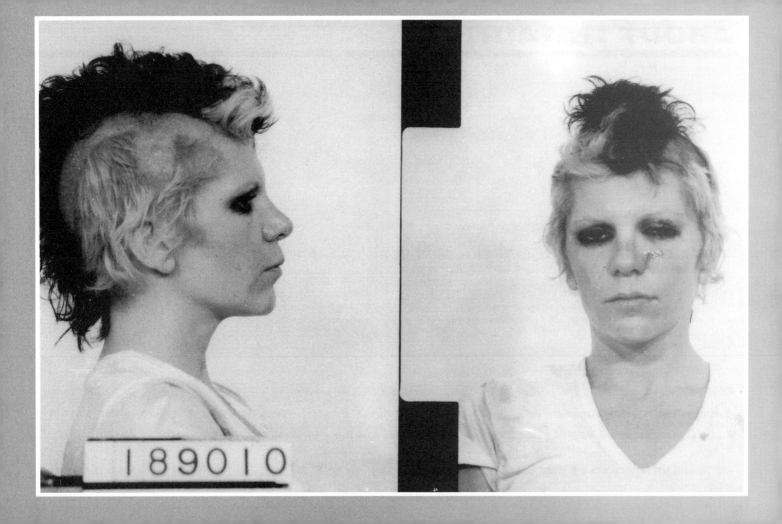

ABOUT THE AUTHOR

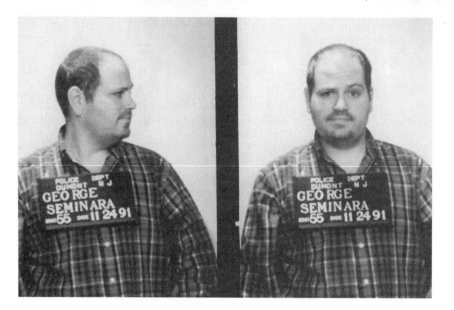

George Seminara is an artist, photographer, and filmmaker. He has worked as a store clerk, stunt man, projectionist, garbageman, cinematographer, and toy designer. He has directed music videos for such artists as The Ramones, Big Audio Dynamite, and Live. His video for Snow's "Informer" was the number-one video worldwide in 1993.

Mr. Seminara lives on the Lower East Side of Manhattan with his wife, two cats, and a pit bull terrier named Daisy.